do it **NOW** *do it* **FAST** *do it* **RIGHT**®

Kitchen

Makeovers

do it **NOW** *do it* **FAST** *do it* **RIGHT**®

Kitchen

Makeovers

The Taunton Press

The Taunton Press
Inspiration for hands-on living®

The Taunton Press, Inc., 63 South Main Street, PO Box 5506, Newtown, CT 06470-5506

e-mail: tp@taunton.com

PRODUCED BY SPOOKY CHEETAH PRESS

WRITER AND PROJECT MANAGER: Rick Peters

EDITOR: Brian Fitzgerald

SERIES DESIGN: Lori Wendin

LAYOUT: Art Gecko Studios!

ILLUSTRATOR: Charles Lockhart

PHOTOGRAPHER: Christopher Vendetta

COVER PHOTOGRAPHERS: All cover photographs by Christopher Vendetta, except

front cover main photo © Tim Street-Porter

Taunton's Do It Now/Do It Fast/Do It Right® is a trademark of
The Taunton Press, Inc., registered in the U.S. Patent and Trademark Office.

LIBRARY OF CONGRESS CATALOGING-IN-PUBLICATION DATA

Kitchen makeovers.

    p. cm. -- (Do it now/do it fast/do it right)

  ISBN 1-56158-726-5

  1. Kitchens--Remodeling--Amateurs' manuals. I. Taunton Press. II. Series.

TH4816.3.K58K578 2005

643'.4--dc22

                        2004024692

Printed in the United States of America

10 9 8 7 6 5 4 3 2 1

The following manufacturers/names appearing in *Kitchen Makeovers* are trademarks: Behr®, Black & Decker®, Black & Decker Bulls-Eye™, Bosch™, Bostitch®, Bucket Boss®, Delta®, Dewalt®, Hercules®, Hercules Sta Put®, Makita®, Quick Grip®, Stabila®, Stanley®, Stanley PowerLock®, Stanley Max Steel™, Zircon®.

Acknowledgments

We're grateful to the manufacturers and their representatives who contributed photographs and products shown on these pages: Sara Hoblik (Amerock Corporation), Cooper Smith (Daltile Corporation), Rob Jenkins (Rev-A-Shelf), Nora DePalma (American Standard), Tracy Lewis (Your Other Warehouse), Randy Hicks (Quality Doors), Lisa Cuschleg (Mills Pride), and Jean Jones (Shaw Industries).

Thanks also to the homeowners who allowed us into their homes: Barbara Jones, Kim Irwin, Mike Lahaie, Matt and Kristine Gushee, Cindi Fuller, Debbie Brambilla, Kathy Ware, and Jessica Waldroup.

Contents

Kitchen PROJECTS

Painted Cabinets 16

Brush on a **MAJOR MAKEOVER,** then complete the transformation with new hinges and handles

Tile Backsplash 28

This **TILE TRANSFORMATION** is a great way to brighten up a dull kitchen with color and texture

Cabinet Organizers 38

Make your cabinets work harder with slide-out shelves and other **INGENIOUS ORGANIZERS**

Sink & Faucet Upgrade 50

Transform the centerpiece of your kitchen with a new **SINK & FAUCET**

How to Use This Book

IF YOU'RE INTERESTED IN HOME IMPROVEMENTS that add value and convenience while also enabling you to express your own sense of style, you've come to the right place. **Do It Now/Do It Fast/Do It Right** books are created with an attitude that says "Let's get started!" and an ideal mix of home-improvement inspiration and how-to information. Do It Now books don't skip important steps or force you to guess at what needs to be done to take a project from start to finish.

You'll find that this book has a friendly, easy-to-use format. (See the sample pages shown here.) You'll begin each project knowing exactly what tools and gear you'll need, and what materials to buy at your home center or building-supply outlet. You can get started confidently because every step is illustrated and explained. Along the way, you'll discover plenty of expert advice packed into the margins. For ideas on how to personalize your project, check out the design options pages that follow the step-by-step instructions.

WORK TOGETHER

If you like company when you go to the movies or clean up the kitchen, you'll probably feel the same way about tackling home-improvement projects. The work will go faster, and you'll have a partner to share in the adventure. You'll

Get the TOOLS & GEAR you need. You'll also find out what features and details are important.

DO IT RIGHT tells you what it takes to get top-notch results.

NEED A HAND? gives you great tips that will make the project go smoothly.

WHAT TO BUY helps you put together your project shopping list, so you get all the materials you need.

UPGRADE tells you which materials could add a special touch to your project.

see that some projects really call for another set of
hands to steady a ladder or keep the project going
smoothly. Read through the project you'd like to tackle,
and note where you're most likely to need help.

PLANNING AND PRACTICE PAY OFF

Most of the projects in this book can easily be
completed in a weekend. But the job can take longer
if you don't pay attention to planning and project-
preparation requirements. Check out the conditions
in the area where you'll be working in case repairs are
required before you can begin your project. In the GET SET chapter (beginning
on the next page), you'll find useful information on getting organized and on
many of the tools and materials required for most of the projects in this book.

Your skill and confidence will improve with every project you complete.
But if you're trying a technique for the first time, it's wise to rehearse before
you "go live." This means ordering a little extra in the way of supplies and
materials, and finding a location where you can practice your technique.

DESIGN OPTIONS
Personalize your project with
dimensions, finishes, and
details that suit your space
and sense of style.

DO IT NOW helps
keep your project
on track with timely
advice.

COOL TOOL puts you in
touch with tools that
make the job easier.

STEP BY STEP pages help
you get started, keep
going, and finish the job.
Every step is illustrated
and explained.

Get Set

Take the **RIGHT TOOLS,** add **AFFORDABLE MATERIALS,** and stir in **DESIGN BASICS** for the success recipe for your kitchen makeover

HAVE YOU BEEN PUTTING OFF a kitchen improvement because it seems like too big (and expensive) of a deal? It doesn't have to be—as you'll see step-by-step in these popular kitchen makeover projects. The kitchen is the most remodeled room in the house, and no wonder: As the social center of the home it's usually the most-used space, and it's tops for payback in resale value. Whether you

crave a cabinet upgrade, a new floor, or better lighting, you don't have to spend lots of time and money to reach your goal. Still, because the kitchen is also one of the most complex rooms in a home—with plumbing, electrical, and ventilation systems to consider—you'll find that the tools to make it over can be many and varied.

A kitchen work triangle is a path that connects the refrigerator, sink, and stove. The National Kitchen and Bath Association (NKBA) recommends that no single side of the triangle be more than 9 ft. and that the combined length of the sides not exceed 26 ft.

Work Flow & Storage Space

Some kitchens are a pleasure to work in, others are a chore. The reason? The amount of thought that was given to work flow. This term simply means how meal preparation flows from start to finish: from gathering ingredients from the refrigerator, to prepping vegetables at the sink, to simmering a sauce on a cooktop. In kitchens where this is awkward, little thought was given to work flow, or space limitations did not allow for a more efficient design. The kitchens that work best have well-planned, well-executed layouts. Additionally, a well-laid-out kitchen has storage space that's both plentiful and accessible.

WORK FLOW

In years past, kitchen designers concentrated on just three task or work centers—the cooktop, the sink, and the refrigerator—to form what is commonly called the work triangle. In today's kitchens, this triangle is more like a polygon: cooktop, sink, refrigerator, wall oven, microwave… you get the idea. We've illustrated five common layouts here, along with their work triangles. Besides work flow, it's also important to consider traffic patterns—how your household moves through the kitchen. Be aware that if you alter the work flow in the kitchen, by adding a kitchen island, for instance, you'll alter the traffic flow, too.

1| **ONE-WALL KITCHEN.** A one-wall kitchen is the least efficient kitchen plan because it has all three work centers along a single wall. In small spaces like efficiency apartments or studios, this plan is often the only option. But it does offer one advantage: It can be concealed with sliding or folding doors.

2| **CORRIDOR KITCHEN.** As long as the work centers are grouped closely together, a corridor kitchen can be quite efficient for a single cook. The main disadvantage to this layout is that household traffic typically flows through the space as well.

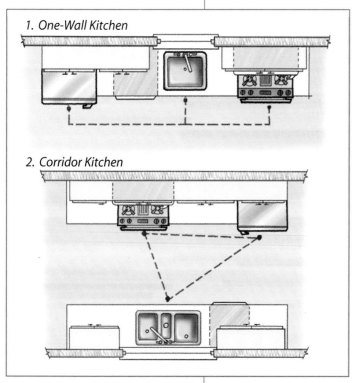

1. One-Wall Kitchen

2. Corridor Kitchen

3. L-Shaped Kitchen

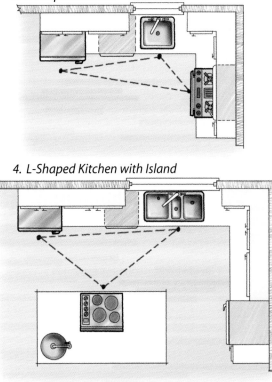

4. L-Shaped Kitchen with Island

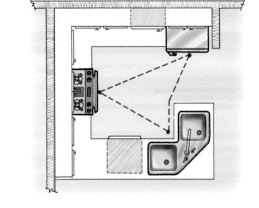

5. U- or G-Shaped Kitchen

3| L-SHAPED KITCHEN. Care must be taken to group the work centers together in this layout. Otherwise, you have an elongated work triangle that creates wasted steps. On the plus side, the L-shaped layout offers generous counter space.

4| L-SHAPED KITCHEN WITH ISLAND. If you add a freestanding island to an L-shaped kitchen, you can tighten up the work triangle as well as increase the storage space. Additionally, if you extend the countertop on one side of the island, you can also create seating for an eating area.

5| U- OR G-SHAPED KITCHEN. The U-shaped layout is generally considered the most efficient kitchen plan. By closely grouping the work centers together, this plan saves steps while surrounding the cook with plenty of counter and storage space. You can turn a U-shaped layout into a G-shaped kitchen by adding an extra wall of cabinets and a countertop that wraps around to become a peninsula.

One of the benefits of a freestanding kitchen island is the added area for food preparation.

STORAGE SPACE

There are many ways to increase kitchen storage space. If you have the room, adding an island is your best bet (see p. 96). Cabinet and cabinet-accessory manufacturers sell units that can turn wasted space (like the unreachable back section of a corner cabinet) into usable space. Tip-out and pull-out bins, along with pull-out shelving, are all excellent ways to shoehorn more storage into a small space (see p. 38). Whatever you choose one thing is for sure: The better organized and more efficient a kitchen is, the more space you'll have for storage.

Before you pick up a hammer or a paintbrush, start by making a list of the projects you want to tackle. At the same time, collect photos of kitchens you like and use these along with paint chips and fabric samples as inspiration to guide your choices in color and materials.

Deciding which materials to use and choosing color schemes can be confusing. Consider seeking professional help from a kitchen designer at a home center or from another design professional, such as an interior designer.

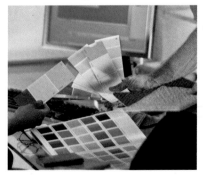

What to Tackle First

If you're planning on doing only one project from this book, just dive right in. If, on the other hand, you want to take on a number of the projects, it's best to complete them in a logical sequence. For example, it wouldn't make sense to install a new floor and then paint the kitchen cabinets. Doing so would create a lot of extra preparation work to protect the new floor from the paint.

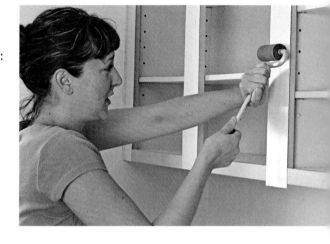

If you do plan to complete multiple projects, consider approaching them in this order:

1| Cabinets

2| Lighting

3| Plumbing

4| Walls

5| Flooring

CABINETS

Painting or refacing cabinets is a messy job. It also requires a lot of space and will effectively shut down your kitchen for a couple of days. It's best to tackle this job first to keep the mess from affecting other projects. Dust from refacing, or paint drips and spills, can be more easily managed in a kitchen that's in the beginning stages of a makeover than one that's in the final steps. It won't matter much if you drip a little paint on a floor that's being re-covered or a sink that's being replaced.

LIGHTING

Once the big messy jobs are complete, you can turn your attention to other tasks, such as lighting. This is a good time to upgrade fixtures so you can shed more light on any remaining projects. Say, for instance, you are going to tile your backsplash. Under-cabinet lighting will brighten this typically dark area,

making it easier to do a professional-quality job. Also, once cabinet doors have been removed and remounted or replaced, there's less chance of accidentally hitting an overhead light. Go ahead and install a new overhead light now if it's part of your makeover.

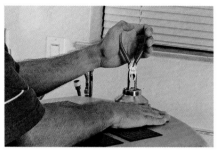

PLUMBING TASKS

Plumbing tasks like replacing a sink or faucet should wait until any cabinet work or painting has been completed. This will prevent these projects from marring the finish on the fixtures. Also, you definitely want to tackle plumbing work before moving on to flooring—especially if you're planning to install laminate flooring—to keep any potential water spills from damaging the new floor.

WALLS

Wall work—whether it's a tile backsplash, a fresh coat of paint, or wallpaper— is best left toward the end of your makeover projects list. This way, if you accidentally ding or damage a wall while working on an earlier project, you can patch and then complete your wall work.

FLOORING

Once all your other makeover projects are complete you can take on the floor. Saving the flooring for last will protect it not only from dust, dirt, and paint spills, but also from scratches and dents created by building materials like sinks and even lighting fixtures. Even your work boots can cause problems: It's surprising what the sole of a boot can pick up during a makeover project. An errant nail or brad stuck in a sole can destroy the top layer of laminate flooring in no time at all.

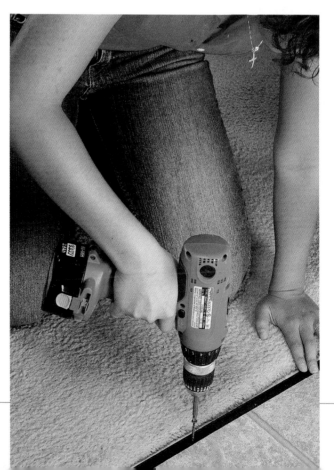

Safety & Codes

Although plumbing and electrical codes may seem to be a nuisance, they're written and enforced to protect you. It's important that you make sure your project adheres to the local codes, so check them before you start. The codes are often available for free or for a small fee from the local building department.

PLUMBING CODES

Plumbing code for a kitchen centers on the sink. In particular, it specifies what types of fixtures and materials are allowed and how the fixtures must be installed. That's why it's important to check before you buy materials. Just because something is available at a hardware store or home center doesn't mean it meets code for installation in your home.

SINK REPLACEMENT. In most areas, a sink can be replaced with another sink of similar size and bowl configuration without a permit, as long as the sink remains in the same location. If the sink has to be moved or the waste lines (drainage) from the bowls do not align with the new sink, the waste lines will need to be replumbed and you'll need to obtain a permit.

FAUCET REPLACEMENT. Faucets can usually be replaced without a permit as long as the new faucet does not require replumbing the supply lines. This is rarely necessary, since flexible supply lines are available at most home centers in a variety of lengths. These lines make it easy to connect existing supply lines to your new faucet.

TRAP REPLACEMENT. There are two main types of sink traps: P-traps and S-traps. A P-trap is designed for drain lines coming out of a wall. S-traps are common when drain lines come up through the floor. S-traps are prone to self-siphoning, which can cause the seal to fail and allow sewer gas into the home. They are prohibited by most codes in new construction. If you have an S-trap and install a new sink, you'll likely need to replace it with a P-trap.

ELECTRICAL CODES

The kitchen is one of the most complicated electrical rooms in the home as it typically requires both 110v and 220v circuits—many of which are dedicated to a single appliance. If you need to move an appliance as part of your makeover, it's best to consult a licensed electrician. Electrical code can be very confusing—and the last thing you want to do is make a mistake where electricity is concerned.

GFCI RECEPTACLES. One of the more critical electrical code requirements for kitchens is that ground fault circuit interrupter (GFCI) receptacles must be installed. GFCI receptacles are safety devices designed to turn off power when a ground fault occurs, such as when an appliance is faulty or an accident happens (like dropping a plugged-in mixer in a sink full of water). If the receptacle is GFCI-protected, it will shut off power almost instantaneously.

GFCI code requirements vary by state and municipality. Some codes require that all receptacles in the kitchen be GFCI. With other codes, it's only those receptacles within a certain distance from the sink or another water-related fixture or appliance, such as a dishwasher.

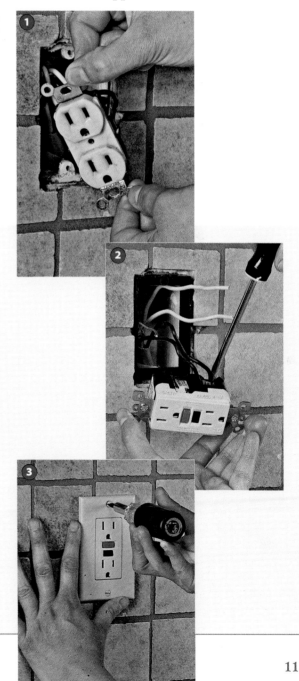

INSTALLING A GFCI RECEPTACLE

1| REMOVE THE OLD RECEPTACLE. Replacing a standard receptacle with a GFCI is simple: It's just a matter of hooking up the new receptacle to the existing wiring. Start by turning off power at the main service panel. Remove the cover-plate screw and cover plate. Unscrew the receptacle mounting screws and set them aside. Gently pull out the old receptacle, loosen each of the screw terminals, and unhook each wire.

2| CONNECT WIRES TO THE NEW RECEPTACLE. Now you can connect the wires to the appropriate screw terminals (or wires) of the GFCI receptacle. Some GFCI receptacles come with screw terminals that you simply use to connect to the existing wires: white wires to the silver terminals and the black wires to the brass terminals. If the receptacle you purchased has wires instead of screw terminals, connect these to the existing wires so that the wire nuts provided match up with the wire colors.

3| MOUNT THE NEW RECEPTACLE. Finally, connect the bare ground wire to the ground lug on the receptacle (or to the green wire), push the receptacle back into the electrical box, and secure it with mounting screws. Add the cover plate and screws, and restore the power.

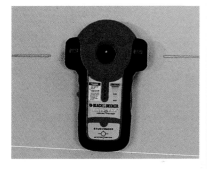
The Right Tools for the Job

OK, so you've decided on a project and you've obtained a permit, if needed. You're ready to go, right? Not quite. Before you get started it's a good idea to look over the project, make a list of the tools you own, and determine what you'll need.

CREATE TOOL KITS

In addition to the specialty tools you'll need for a specific project, consider creating task-specific tool kits. These can be housed in inexpensive plastic toolboxes or buckets. As a homeowner, the three "kits" you'll most likely need are for general carpentry, plumbing, and electrical work. Though there may be some duplication of tools, a kit that's ready to go saves time and ensures you'll have everything you need at your fingertips for a specific job.

RENTAL TOOLS

To save time and money, consider renting some of the more expensive tools needed for a job. Although none of the projects in this book require expensive tools, some of the jobs will go a lot smoother with them. For example, you don't absolutely *need* a power miter saw to cut laminate flooring, but it will make it a whole lot easier to cut perfectly straight ends and miter-cut molding with precision. Likewise, if you're refacing cabinets, you can certainly attach molding with a hammer and some brads. But an air-powered nailer will make quick work of attaching molding, and it will also set the nails at the same time.

General Carpentry Kit

The kit that you'll reach for most often consists of tools commonly used for general carpentry. The bucket organizer shown here slips into an ordinary 5-gallon bucket and holds a surprisingly large number of tools.

CLAW HAMMER. This old standby is needed for general assembly and demolition.

NAIL SETS. You'll need these in a variety of sizes to sink nailheads below the worksurface.

COPING SAW. This saw is used for cutting curved parts, and it's also the tool of choice for making a coped cut for trim.

TAPE MEASURE. Most homeowners find it useful to have both a 12-ft. and a 25-ft. tape on hand.

CORDLESS DRILL/DRIVER. This portable power tool makes drilling holes and driving screws a snap.

LEVELS. A 4-ft. bubble level is best used on large surfaces—the smaller torpedo level works nicely in confined spaces.

COMBINATION SQUARE. This square is used to position parts such as hinges on doors and to check 90-degree and 45-degree angles.

CARPENTER'S PENCIL. There's still nothing better for marking and laying out parts. The pencil's flat design keeps it from rolling off a worksurface.

UTILITY KNIFE & PUTTY KNIFE. A utility knife will handle most cutting and trimming jobs. You'll need a putty knife for filling holes and general patching.

MITER BOX. Use this with a handsaw to cut accurate 45-degree and 90-degree angles. The miter box is most often used for cutting trim and molding to length.

SCREWDRIVERS. Make sure you have a couple of different sizes in both Phillips and flathead. Better yet, consider the newer 4-in-1 screwdriver that holds four bits—two standard and two Phillips—to handle most jobs.

SAFETY GEAR. See DO IT RIGHT on p. 10 for everything you'll need.

Both plumber's putty and Teflon® tape create a seal. But putty works best under sink lips, faucets, and strainers. Teflon tape works best for sealing threaded parts, such as connections between shut-off valves and flexible supply lines.

Quick-action-style clamps allow you to position the clamp and close the jaws with one hand—any other style clamp requires both hands.

Basic Plumbing Kit

It's always good to have a basic plumbing kit on hand for a project, but it really shines in an emergency. When water starts leaking out of a cabinet, the last thing you want to do is search through a toolbox for an adjustable wrench. The following tools will make a good start for a plumbing kit.

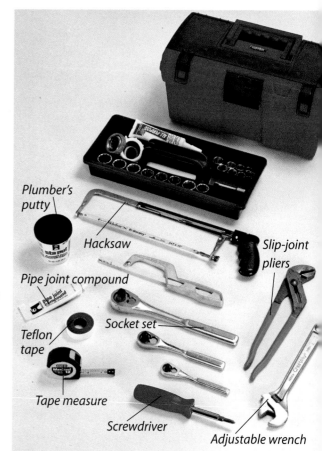

Plumber's putty

Hacksaw

Slip-joint pliers

Pipe joint compound

Socket set

Teflon tape

Tape measure

Screwdriver

Adjustable wrench

ADJUSTABLE WRENCH. The 4-in. and 8-in. sizes can handle the loosening and tightening of nuts and bolts of nearly any size.

SCREWDRIVERS. A Phillips and flathead or a 4-in-1 screwdriver will handle general assembly/disassembly.

SLIP-JOINT PLIERS. These pliers ratchet open to loosen or tighten larger nuts and slip-joint fittings.

SOCKET SET. The standard set with various-size ratchets can handle many assembly/disassembly jobs.

PLUMBER'S PUTTY. You'll need putty for sealing fixtures such as sinks and faucets.

HACKSAW. You'll need a hacksaw to cut metal and plastic pipe to length.

PIPE JOINT COMPOUND. This seals threaded parts and compression fittings. It's useful for tight spaces where using Teflon tape isn't possible.

TEFLON TAPE. Use Teflon tape for sealing threaded parts without the mess of pipe joint compound.

TAPE MEASURE. Use this for measuring when cutting pipe to length and for identifying part sizes for replacement.

Basic Electrical Kit

As with the plumbing kit, an electrical kit is handy for both emergencies and basic electrical projects.

DIAGONAL CUTTER. This is used for cutting wire and cable to length.

WIRE STRIPPERS. You'll need these to strip insulation off the ends of wire in preparation for making electrical connections.

NEEDLE-NOSE PLIERS. Use needle-nose pliers for twisting and bending wire to make electrical connections.

CIRCUIT TESTER. This is useful for checking for power. Simple versions have a single lamp to signify power/no power. More complex versions indicate electrical polarity.

SCREWDRIVERS. Use these for assembly and disassembly, including making connections on screw-type terminals.

LINESMAN PLIERS. These are a hybrid of a diagonal cutter and regular pliers. The inside edges of the jaws are sharpened to cut wire and the flat ends are for gripping, bending, and twisting wire.

WIRE NUTS. These are useful for making quick connections between two or more wires. Various sizes are available to handle different gauge wire.

ELECTRICIAN'S TAPE. This is used to insulate electrical parts from each other.

FUSE PULLER. You'll need a fuse puller to safely pull fuses (many older houses have fuses instead of breakers) to disconnect power to a circuit.

MULTITESTER OR MULTIMETER. This is an advanced measuring tool capable of displaying voltage, current, and resistance.

Wire nuts

Multimeter

Circuit tester

Diagonal cutter

Fuse puller

Electrician's tape

Linesman pliers

Wire stripper

SETTING UP A SIMPLE WORKSTATION

Virtually any project you take on will require a worksurface. To make a simple workstation, use a pair of sawhorses to form a foundation and lay a 3/4-in.-thick piece of plywood on top. A 2-ft. by 4-ft. piece works well for most jobs. For a larger surface, consider using a hollow-core door. Secure the top to the sawhorses with clamps. For super-quick setups, consider using quick-action-style clamps (see NEED A HAND, left).

Painted Cabinets

Brush on a MAJOR MAKEOVER, then complete the transformation with new hinges and handles

I F YOU'RE FAMILIAR WITH THE WORKING END of a paintbrush and roller, then you already have the skills to give your kitchen one of the most dramatic makeovers possible—at the lowest possible cost. Go lighter or brighter, cool it down, or spice it up—with color alone, you can give your whole kitchen a new look. Replace the pulls, handles, and hinges, and you'll create an even greater impact. Be sure to clean your surfaces thoroughly first, then apply the paint, attach your new hardware, and get ready for compliments.

SAND THE SURFACES   **APPLY THE PAINT**   **REMOUNT THE DOORS**   **ADD NEW HARDWARE**

▶ DO IT RIGHT

To get a smooth, roller-mark-free finish on painted surfaces, use the "striking off" technique the pros use. After you've rolled the entire surface with paint, go back and position the roller at the top of the surface. Then roll it all the way down the length in one continuous stroke. Start back at the top, right next to the area you just rolled. Repeat as needed to strike off the whole surface.

❖ COOL TOOL

If you're sanding your cabinets by hand, use a sanding block to evenly distribute pressure. A sanding block is easy to make: Just wrap a third of a sheet of sandpaper around a 5-in. section of a 1x4.

Tools & Gear

If you've done any painting in your home, you'll probably have most of the tools you need to paint cabinets. The only specialty tools involved are for removing and adding hardware.

CLEANING SUPPLIES. To get a good paint bond, you'll need to clean your cabinets thoroughly. A bucket and stiff bristle brush coupled with some trisodium phosphate (TSP) work well to remove built-up dirt. Be sure to wear rubber gloves and eye protection when working with TSP.

PAINTER'S TAPE, DROP CLOTHS, LATEX GLOVES & RAGS. Keep paint off walls, floors, and countertops with painter's tape and drop cloths—keep it off your hands by wearing gloves. You'll also want rags on hand to handle spills.

STEPLADDER. Reach the tops of wall cabinets with a stepladder when cleaning, priming, or painting.

AWL. The sharp point of an awl lets you indent screw locations for hardware. The indent also serves as a starting point for a drill bit.

SCREWDRIVER OR CORDLESS DRILL/DRIVER. You can remove and install doors and hardware with a screwdriver, but a drill/driver will speed up the job.

SELF-CENTERING DRILL BIT. This nifty drill accessory makes it easy to drill perfectly centered mounting holes for hinges.

COMBINATION SQUARE. The square's adjustable blade makes it the perfect tool for positioning hardware quickly and accurately.

RANDOM-ORBIT SANDER & 150-GRIT SANDPAPER. Cabinets need to be roughed up to give primer and paint something to "bite" into. A random-orbit sander works best since it won't leave tiny swirl marks like an orbital sander might.

SMALL ROLLER & PAINT TRAY. The fastest way to apply paint to cabinets is to roll it on. A small 3-in. to 4-in. foam roller is ideal for this.

FOAM BRUSHES. Even if you use a roller, you'll still need a 2-in. foam brush to handle edges and details—like the molded edges of raised panels.

PUTTY KNIFE. This tool is useful for filling holes with putty and scraping away old paint.

WHAT'S DIFFERENT?

Sealers (often referred to as sanding sealers) are intended for use on bare wood only. Primers, on the other hand, can be applied to previously painted wood. Primers do a couple of things: They seal any open pores and help lock in stains. They also provide a better foundation for new paint because they are formulated to adhere or "bite" into the old paint better than a new coat of paint can.

What to Buy

The supplies you'll need to paint your cabinets are inexpensive. What can cost a bit, though, is the hardware. Your total price tag will depend on how many pieces you need and the cost per item.

1| PUTTY OR FILLER. You'll need this to fill in the holes used to mount your old hardware. Solvent-based fillers are the best since they shrink less and dry quicker than water-based fillers. Ask for help before buying though—not all solvent-based fillers accept paint well.

2| PRIMER & PAINT. To choose a primer and paint for your cabinets, ask for help at your local hardware store or home center. The type you use will depend on the existing finish. Oil-based primers usually bond better with old finishes than water-based primers do—but they also have a strong odor and take longer to dry. You can cover either with latex enamel paint. Enamel will create a tougher finish that's more resistant to staining and chipping than regular latex paint will.

3| NEW HARDWARE. You'll need one pair of hinges for every door and either a pull or knob for each drawer and door. This can get expensive—especially if you choose high-end hardware. But since most hardware stores and home centers have pulls and knobs that cost less than two bucks apiece, you can keep hardware costs below $100 with some wise shopping. If you like the current position of your knobs and pulls, try to find new hardware that matches up with the old mounting holes. If you find suitable hardware, you can skip filling in the old holes in the drawers and doors with putty.

TYPES OF HINGES

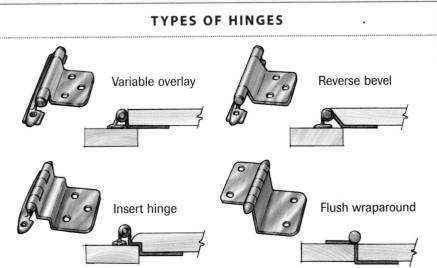

Variable overlay

Reverse bevel

Insert hinge

Flush wraparound

WHAT CAN GO WRONG?

Though many cabinet door hinges are similar in appearance, they are not all the same. Make sure you know what type you need before purchasing new hinges. If you want to keep the same type, take an old hinge with you to the store to help find a replacement. If you're thinking about upgrading your hardware, now is a good time to do it.

▶ **DO IT RIGHT**

It's very easy to mix up doors when it comes time to reinstall them. To prevent this, scratch a position code into each door under the hinge location with an awl before painting. This way, even if the code gets covered with paint, you'll still be able to read it.

✳ **WHAT'S DIFFERENT?**

Wood cabinets usually accept paint well. But cabinets with doors, drawers, and face frames that are covered with any kind of plastic laminate (such as melamine) *cannot* be painted. If you're not sure which type you have, check by brushing paint in an inconspicuous spot—like the back of a door. Once it's dry, scrape the paint with your fingernail. If the door is covered with plastic laminate, the paint will flake right off.

Prep for Painting

1 **REMOVE DOORS, DRAWERS & HARDWARE.** Since you'll want to reinstall the doors and drawers later in their original locations, label each part. Drawers can usually be removed by pulling them out and lifting up to disengage the rollers. Label each drawer by writing a position code on masking tape stuck to the drawer bottom. See DO IT RIGHT, left, for labeling doors. Use a screwdriver or cordless drill/driver to remove all knobs, pulls, hinges, and catches.

2 **CLEAN ALL SURFACES.** Before you reach for your paint, take the time to prepare the cabinet surfaces so you'll get the best paint bond possible. This is a crucial step since paint can't bond with dirty surfaces. Start by cleaning the doors, drawer fronts, and face frames with a solution of TSP and water. Follow the manufacturer's recommendations for the right mix. TSP is a strong detergent, so wear rubber gloves and eye protection as you clean. A stiff bristle brush will help scour away stubborn kitchen dirt. Allow the parts to dry overnight.

3 **SAND GLOSSY SURFACES.** When the cabinet parts are completely dry, sand all surfaces lightly with 150-grit open-coat sandpaper wrapped around a sanding block. You don't need to sand down to bare wood—in fact, that's the last thing you want to do. All you want to do here is scuff the surface enough to give the paint something to "bite" into. A random-orbit sander will make quick work of this tedious job.

4 **FILL HARDWARE HOLES.** Next, if you're not reusing the hardware mounting holes, fill these holes and imperfections (dings, dents, etc.) by pressing putty or filler into the holes with a putty knife. (If  you're reusing hardware, leave the holes for the screws unfilled.) Apply enough putty so it's a bit proud of the surface. After the putty has dried for the recommended amount of time, use a sanding block to sand the putty flush with the surface.

1

2

3

4

If you plan on reusing existing hardware holes, you may find one that has been stripped. To solve this problem, just dip the end of one or two wooden toothpicks in glue and insert into the hole. Trim off the excess with your utility knife and drive in the screw. The screw threads will "bite" into the toothpicks for a solid grip.

▶ DO IT RIGHT

A simple drilling jig is just a ¼-in. piece of wood. Cleats on both faces help position the jig for drilling. Pick a location for the hardware, then measure the distance up from the bottom of the door or drawer and offset from the adjacent edge. Transfer these measurements to the jig, then drill the desired-size mounting hole at this spot. Position the jig on the corner of a door or drawer so the cleats butt up against the edges of the part. Drill through the hole in the jig and your hardware will be perfectly aligned.

Prime, Paint & Finish

5 **MASK OFF SURFACES.** Before you paint the face frames, you'll likely need to mask off adjacent areas, such as walls, countertops, and the floor. Painter's tape lets you mask off large areas quickly. Use drop cloths to protect the countertops and floor.

6 **PRIME ALL SURFACES.** Using a small foam roller, prime the backs of the doors. While they're drying, prime the cabinet face frames, drawer fronts, and the sides of any end cabinets. Once the doors are dry (usually within an hour or two), flip them over and prime the front.

7 **PAINT ALL SURFACES.** After the primer has dried overnight, use the same procedure to paint the face frames, doors, drawer fronts, and cabinet sides with the finish coat. If you're painting dark cabinets a light color, you'll likely discover that you need two to three coats for good coverage. If you do need multiple coats, consult the recommended drying times on the can of paint.

8 **INSTALL NEW HINGES.** An accurate way to install hinges—if you're not using the existing holes—is with a combination square. Determine how far in you want the hinges from the cabinet edge. Set the blade of the square to that distance and mark it. By using this method to position each hinge, all hinges—and cabinet doors—will be in alignment. Use a self-centering bit in the drill/driver to drill pilot holes, then secure the hinges to the doors with screws.

9 **INSTALL THE DOORS & ADD PULLS AND KNOBS.** Now you can mount the doors to the cabinets. Center one door at a time in the opening then drill mounting holes with a self-centering bit, using the hinge as your guide. Drive the supplied screws into the holes to secure the doors to the cabinets. Repeat for the remaining doors, taking care to align them with each other. All that's left is to add the hardware. Use a drilling jig (see DO IT RIGHT, left) to guide your drill bit. When you've drilled all the holes, attach the knobs and pulls with the screws provided.

5 **6**

7 **8**

9

Give your fingers something to "smile" about every time you pull on one of these fun-shaped knobs. Molded in smooth metal, these intriguing shapes blend utility with whimsy.

The kitchen is a great place to mix and match—as long as different looks complement, not compete. Here, warm oak cabinets frame the food prep area while their sage-painted cousins define the window wall and sink.

A dash of color or an unexpected texture or shape can add an engaging dimension to an otherwise ho-hum kitchen. You can define a part of the kitchen, accent an asset, or hide flaws, all with a few sweeps of the brush or roller. You might not think that something as small as a knob can have such a large impact on the overall look of a kitchen—but it can. New hardware is one of the easiest ways to spruce up your cabinets.

File this entry under "bright ideas." These curved pulls evoke memories of card catalogues from the libraries of our youth. The labels allow you to easily locate whatever it is you're searching for—and you won't need the Dewey decimal system to find it!

Get a handle on new textures for adding visual interest. The surprise of fine leather (stitched over stainless steel frames) will make every drawer opening something special for the eye and hand.

Give your cabinets an antique look that doesn't take years to achieve. A sand-through finish like the one on this cabinet door will give your kitchen a warm, lived-in feel.

An off-white paint creates the perfect creamy tone that will lighten up a kitchen and accept almost any style of hardware. Leaving the cabinets light lets you introduce color to the walls, countertop, and floor.

Bring a subtle touch of the outdoors to the kitchen with nature-themed pulls and handles, like these engraved metal beauties.

A glazed finish, textured glass, and gleaming pewter knobs set the stage for showing off collections—and the cabinets themselves.

Hand-hammered surfaces combine with fanciful flowers to produce authentic, rustic knobs and pulls. Accents like these can add just the right touch to your kitchen.

For splashes of color and design, ceramics really shine. Whether patterns or solids, pastels or punchy brights, they're a great option for bringing cachet to cabinets.

Warm wood and cool metal give a double-texture appeal to these handles. The wood softens a contemporary room, while the metal adds a modern touch to traditional decor.

Tile Backsplash

This **TILE TRANSFORMATION** is a great way to brighten up a dull kitchen with color and texture

ERE'S A PROJECT that does triple duty in function, form, and ease of accomplishment. A tile backsplash not only protects your walls from water, grease, and grime, but it can also add visual punch to a ho-hum kitchen. What's more, it's one of the simplest tiling jobs you can take on, so it's a great project for beginners. Just stroll the tile aisle of your local home center to browse the myriad colors, patterns, and textures available. Then use the detailed steps here to create a new accent for your kitchen that only *looks* difficult and expensive.

INSTALL BACKER BOARD   APPLY THE MORTAR   SET THE TILES   APPLY THE GROUT

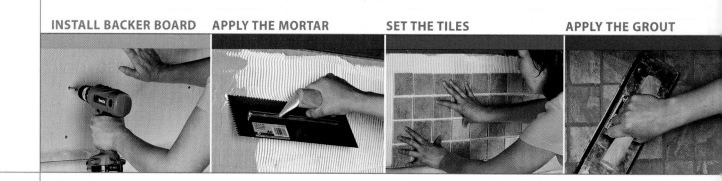

▶ **DO IT RIGHT**

Between the backer board and the tile, tiling a backsplash will add $1/2$ in. or more to the thickness of your wall. This means anything mounted in an electrical box needs to be extended in order to be flush with the tile. That's where box extenders come in. These plastic rectangles are available in various thicknesses.

◑ **NEED A HAND?**

Gravity works against you when you're tiling a wall. To fight gravity's pull on the tiles, use strips of masking tape to help hold tiles in place until the mortar sets up.

Tools & Gear

There are three distinct types of tools you'll need to install tile: tile-cutting tools, mortar tools, and grout tools. Which ones you'll use will depend on the type of tile you're installing and the obstacles you'll need to work around.

NOTCHED TROWEL. Use this tool to apply thin-set mortar. The evenly spaced notches on the edges range from $1/8$ in. to $3/8$ in. in size.

GROUT FLOAT. This rubber-faced tool is similar to a notched trowel and is used to force grout into the spaces between the tiles. When held at an angle, it's also useful for scraping off excess grout.

SPONGE & RAGS. You'll need a sponge to wipe off the grout after it's dried to a haze and clean rags to buff the tiles clean after sponging.

TILE SPACERS. Cross-shaped plastic tile spacers can be inserted between each tile to ensure consistent spacing and even grout joints between the tiles. Spacers are available in different sizes to create varying-width joint lines.

TILE CUTTER. You can easily cut straight lines on smooth, glazed tiles with a tile cutter.

TILE NIPPERS. These pliers-like tools remove tiny bits of tile by nipping away at the edges.

RUBBER-FACED MALLET. This is the best tool for setting or "bedding" tile in thin-set mortar.

STUD FINDER & CORDLESS DRILL/DRIVER. Use a stud finder to locate the wall studs and a drill/driver to drive the special screws that secure the backer board to the studs.

MASKING TAPE, MESH TAPE & DROP CLOTH. Seal electrical receptacles with masking tape, and use mesh tape to hide seams in the backer board. A drop cloth will protect your counters.

SMALL BRUSH. It's easiest to apply grout sealer to thin grout lines with a small brush.

UPGRADE

Specialty "decorator" tiles that are colorful, embossed, or made from small pieces (mosaics) can be very expensive. Instead of covering an entire backsplash with these, savvy homeowners sprinkle them throughout a backsplash as an inexpensive accent or to add a spark of color.

What to Buy

1| BACKER BOARD. Often referred to as cement board, backer board is a thin sheet of cement-like material that you attach to the wall to create a smooth surface for the tile. It also prevents the water in thin-set mortar from damaging your wall. Backer board comes in 1/4-in. and 1/2-in. thicknesses. Quarter-inch board is much easier to work with because it can be cut by first scribing a line and then snapping it to length. The thicker 1/2-in. type must be cut with a power saw fitted with a masonry or diamond-coated blade.

2| BACKER BOARD FASTENERS. Backer board manufacturers recommend securing the board to your wall with corrosion-resistant screws or nails with a minimum length of 1 1/4 in. A good option is to use ribbed countersinking screws, which are designed to self-drill to the depth necessary for the screw to sit flush with the backer board.

3| TILE. Ceramic tile is the most common type of tile used in backsplashes. It cuts easily and is available in an array of colors, patterns, and textures. Porcelain is a special type of ceramic tile that is much harder and, therefore, harder to cut. If you're planning to install porcelain tile, plan also to buy or rent a motorized tile saw. As a general rule, wall tiles look best when they're 4 in. square or smaller. Mosaic tiles—in which a web-like backing is adhered to the back of small tiles to ensure uniform spacing—also look great on a backsplash. When you purchase tile, make sure to select boxes of tiles that were made in the same batch. Look for identical lot and shade numbers marked on the sides of each box of tiles to ensure uniform color and overall appearance. You'll also need some bullnose tiles, which have one rounded, glazed side, for the edges and top of your backsplash.

4| THIN-SET MORTAR. Thin-set mortar is the "glue" that bonds tile to a backer board or wall. You can buy it in dry form and mix it with water into an oatmeal-like consistency, or buy it premixed, in which case all you need to do is trowel it on. Premixed mortar tends to be stickier than mixed mortar and works especially well for wall tile. Its extra grip helps fight gravity.

5| GROUT. You'll find grout labeled as either sanded or unsanded. Use unsanded grout to fill fine gaps less than 1/16 in. wide. For wider gaps, use grout that has sand added to it to serve as filler. Grout colors are almost as varied as the tiles themselves.

6| GROUT SEALER. Grout is porous and will stain if not sealed. Consult the grout label for the recommended sealer.

◆ **DO IT NOW**

Wall tile is designed to be installed level and plumb. Don't depend on your eye for this. Instead, mark vertical and horizontal reference lines on the backer board before tiling. If you have a window above your sink, it's best to draw a centerline on the sink or window as a starting point for the tile. This way you'll end up with an equal amount of tiles on both sides.

❂ **DO IT FAST**

Many wall tiles have built-in nibs on their sides that space the tiles apart for consistent grout lines. For tiles that don't have these, you'll need to use tile spacers. These plastic pieces let you quickly position tiles with uniform spacing.

Test, then Tile

1 **INSTALL BACKER BOARD.** To prepare your backsplash for tile, you'll need to attach a layer of backer board. Start by locating and marking the wall studs with a stud finder. Next, using the screws recommended by the backer board manufacturer, attach the board to the wall studs. If there are any seams, cover them with mesh tape. Apply a thin layer of thin-set mortar over the tape with a trowel. Draw reference lines on the backer board to mark your starting point (see DO IT NOW, left).

2 **TEST THE PATTERN.** Regardless of the type of tile you've chosen for the backsplash, it's always a good idea to make a test run "dry." This means laying out the sheets of tile on your countertop or worksurface to check how they'll look. You'll often find color, shading, or pattern differences that you'll want to adjust. This is an especially important step when you're working with variegated tiles (like the mosaic tiles shown here), which you'll want to mix and match to get the most pleasing pattern overall.

3 **APPLY MORTAR.** When you're happy with the tile pattern, use the notched trowel to spread the mortar onto the backer board. Most makers of thin-set mortar suggest a 1/4-in. notch for tiles 12 in. or less in length; others suggest a 3/16-in. notch—see the mortar and tile packaging for recommended size. Spread the mortar over an area about 2 ft. square. Avoid working the mortar excessively. What you're looking for here is a consistent layer with no bare spots.

4 **POSITION A ROW OF TILES.** Now you can begin to lay tiles. Start by positioning the first tile along your marked starting point or reference lines. Since the mortar will probably obscure these, use a level to make sure the first tiles are in alignment. Press down slightly as you lay the tile to force it into the mortar. If you are using spacers, install one between each tile as you place the tiles on the wall.

1

2

3

4

Nip, Grout & Clean

5 **INSTALL PARTIAL & SPECIALTY TILES.**
Place a full tile in the leftover space at the end of a row and scribe a line on the tile where it needs to be cut. Use a tile cutter or motorized tile saw to cut any partial tiles in a straight line. Curved or notched tile can be cut

using a tile nipper. Exercise patience here: If you try to nip off too large a piece, you can end up snapping off much more than you wanted. Install partial tiles as you do full tiles. Finish off the sides or tops of the tiled area with bullnose or other specialty tiles.

6 **APPLY GROUT.** Once the tile is in place, and you've waited the recommended time for the mortar to set (typically overnight), you can apply grout. If you've used tile spacers, remove these first by prying them out with an awl or pulling them out with pliers. Mix grout if necessary and then spread it over the tiles with a grout float. Press down on the float to force the grout into the joints.

7 **SQUEEGEE OFF THE EXCESS.** To remove the excess grout, hold the float at an angle so that the bottom edge acts like a squeegee. Skew the float diagonally as you wipe it across the tiles. This way, the edge of the float can safely span the joints without falling in and squeezing out the grout from the joint. Continue working the area until most of the grout has been removed. Wipe down the float, then go over the area one more time with the float held nearly vertical to scrape off as much grout as possible.

8 **CLEAN THE TILES.** Remove the remaining grout with a wet sponge. Have a large bucket on hand and refill it with clean water often. Just as you did with the float, wipe the sponge diagonally over the tiles. Wipe over each grout joint only once—repeated wiping can pull the grout right out of the joint. After the grout has dried to a haze (which takes less than an hour), use a soft cloth to buff away the grout film.

5

6

7

8

The not-so-humble backsplash

protects the wall from liquids and grime, of course, but it does so much more when the material is versatile tile. Use it to punch up the color in your kitchen, extend the decorating theme of the room, or add a special texture to a plain space. Whatever your taste or budget, there are lots of tiles to choose from.

An embossed tile backsplash blends durability with a touch of elegance.

Thanks to the soft and varied tones of the backsplash tile, the eye is led not to the cooktop or microwave, but to a swath of texture and color.

Fond of flowers? Crazy for critters? A fan of fine art? You can find theme tiles to suit just about any interest. They're just perfect for making a personal statement.

An otherwise plain expanse of solid-surface material gains bold impact from an inset border of background and accent tiles.

With specialty tiles like this raised border, the rustic tones of subtly patterned tile seem more vivid. Borders also draw the eye and define backsplash spaces.

For classic old-world elegance, hand-painted tiles add a rich look (sometimes with prices to match). Use them sparingly for dramatic effect, or concentrate your makeover dollars and enjoy their beauty everywhere.

Glimmering clear-glass tiles are 4-in. squares of fun. The color comes from glaze bonded to the back. They're a bit pricey, but are clearly super as accent tiles.

Cabinet Organizers

Make your cabinets work harder with slide-out shelves and other
INGENIOUS ORGANIZERS

KITCHEN STORAGE SPACE IS LIKE MONEY: For most people, there can never be too much. But there are easy ways to make the most of what you have—without knocking out walls or adding cabinets. A great way to maximize your space is with pull-out bins and shelves. These handy helpers install quickly and yield a lifetime of benefits. If you're tired of getting down on your knees to access those hard-to-reach items, make your kitchen work better and smarter. Invest just a little time and money now, and you'll wonder how you ever managed without these essential extras.

MARK MOUNTING HOLES   **DRILL MOUNTING HOLES**   **ATTACH SLIDING RAILS**   **INSTALL PULL-OUTS**

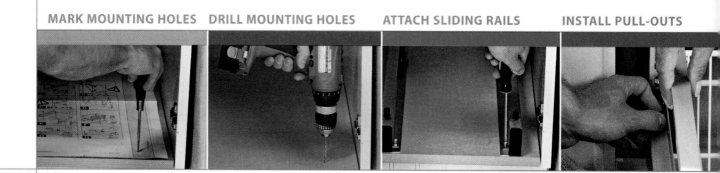

Tools & Gear

The tools you'll need to install cabinet organizers are simple and few. Odds are you have most of them on hand already.

TAPE MEASURE. You'll need one of these to measure cabinets before ordering organizers and then to place them inside the cabinets. A 12-in. tape is long enough, and its small size makes it easy to use inside cabinets.

AWL. This is the perfect tool for marking hole locations for screws. Not only does it mark the location, but its sharp point also makes a depression that serves as a starting point for a drill bit.

DRILL & BITS. To mount an organizer inside a cabinet, you'll need a drill and bits to drill holes for the mounting screws. A small drill bit set is all that's needed.

SCREWDRIVERS. You'll find that it's generally easier to install mounting screws inside a cabinet with a screwdriver than with a drill/driver because of the limited space. Have both standard and Phillips head screwdrivers on hand.

LEVEL. One of the best ways to keep a shelf or bin sliding smoothly is to mount it level in the first place. A small torpedo level works best in the confined interior of a cabinet.

WOOD FILLER OR PUTTY. If you have old hardware holes to fill, or inadvertently drill a hole in the wrong spot, use putty to fill the hole. On finished cabinets, the crayon-like wax fillers work best. Just rub the tip over the hole to fill it and wipe away any excess with a clean cloth.

PUTTY KNIFE. A putty knife is also a necessity if you want to fill in holes properly. For example, if you remove the hinges from a door to attach the door to a pull-out bracket, you'll want to fill the old hinge-mounting screws in the cabinet.

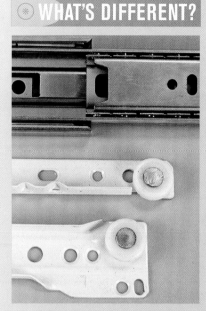

What to Buy

The cabinet organizers you buy will depend on which cabinets you want to organize, the size of the cabinets, and the organizers available. The two most commonly used organizers are pull-out bins and pull-out shelving.

1| PULL-OUT BINS. Pull-out bins are generally the easiest type of organizer to fit and install. That's because most attach to the inside bottom of the cabinet. All you have to do is find a bin that's smaller than your cabinet opening—even by a few inches. Pull-out bins are available with one, two, or three bins. The three-bin units typically have triangle-shaped bins and are used as recycling centers.

2| PULL-OUT SHELVING. Buying pull-out shelving can be tricky because some shelving units are adjustable over a certain width and others aren't. Keep in mind that the dimensions of the unit you buy must match your cabinet. Most shelving units ride on separate slides that are mounted to the sides of the cabinet interior. You can find preassembled double-shelf units that attach to the bottom of the cabinet, but you can't adjust the shelf height as you can with separate shelves. The downside to separate shelves is that if they aren't mounted level and parallel to each other, the shelf may bind. Pull-out shelving is available with shallow wood drawers, plastic-coated wire baskets, chrome wire baskets, and even wicker baskets.

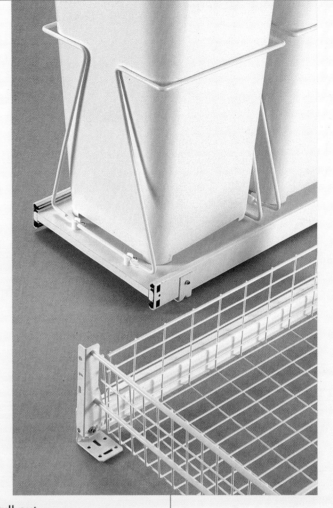

DO IT RIGHT

Most cabinet accessories are adjustable only over a very small range. So it's critical that the accessory to be installed matches the cabinet space. Before you even start looking at cabinet organizers, measure the openings of all the cabinets you want to organize. Measure each opening carefully, positioning your tape measure inside the face frames (if applicable) or inside the cabinet. Take each measurement a couple of times to double-check for accuracy. If possible, have someone help you take the measurements. It's easier to read the tape if you're not holding both ends.

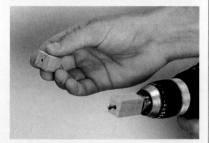

A wooden stop will keep you from drilling through a cabinet part and ruining it. Using the same bit you'll use to drill your mounting hole, drill a hole through a short scrap of wood (say a 2-in.-long section of a 1x4). Then cut the scrap to length so it fits over the drill bit, exposing only the length of bit needed to drill to the desired depth.

Want the convenience of a pull-out bin without the hassle of first opening a cabinet door? Most cabinet-accessory manufacturers sell optional brackets that allow you to attach the existing cabinet door directly to the pull-out mechanism. With these brackets installed, you simply pull out the door to access the contents.

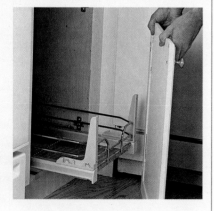

Install Bins

1 **REMOVE DOORS.** Removing the cabinet doors will give you some extra room to work in the confined space inside a cabinet. Have a helper steady each door while you remove the hinge-mounting screws with a screwdriver. Set the doors aside. Thread the screws back into the mounting holes so you won't lose them. For frameless cabinets that use 32mm hinges, you can often simply loosen a screw and press a release lever to disconnect the hinge flap from the side of the cabinet.

2 **LOCATE MOUNTING HOLES WITH A TEMPLATE.** The first step in mounting a pull-out bin is to locate and mark the center of the cabinet with a tape measure and pencil. Then position the manufacturer-

supplied template so it's centered on this mark. Mark the mounting holes in the bottom of the cabinet by pressing through the paper template with an awl. This will leave a small depression in the cabinet bottom that will make it easy to start your drill bit at the proper screw locations.

3 **DRILL HOLES FOR THE MOUNTING MECHANISM.** Once you've marked the hole locations, remove the template, chuck the recommended size bit in your drill, and drill the holes.

4 **ATTACH THE RAILS TO THE CABINET.** Use the screws provided to secure the bin base or bin rails (as shown here) to the cabinet base. If separate rails are used, measure between them in a couple of places to make sure they're parallel. If they're not, loosen the screws, adjust as necessary, and retighten.

5 **ADD THE PULL-OUT MECHANISM.** Extend the rails as far as they will go and align the pull-out mechanism with their ends. A helper can make the job much easier. In most cases, the mechanism will have a set of tabs that fit in openings in the rails. Once in place, test the operation to make sure it's smooth. Finally, place the bin or bins inside the mechanism.

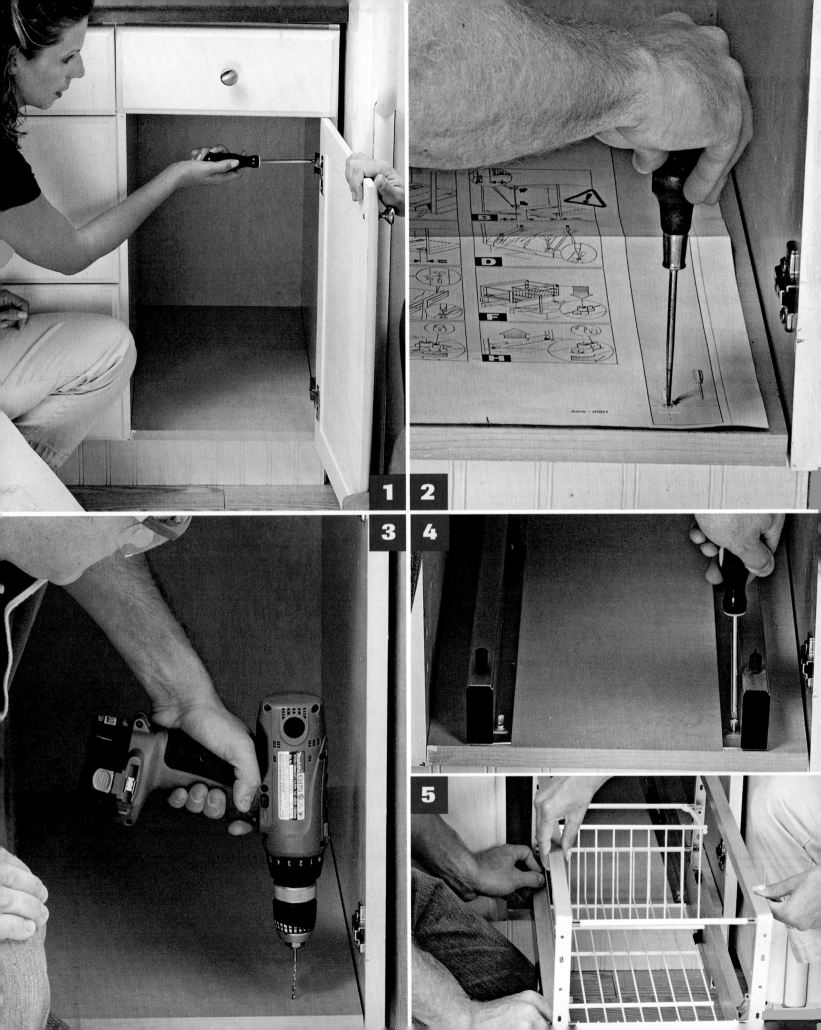

1 **2**

3 **4**

5

Pull-out shelves can bind if the brackets are not level with each other or if they aren't parallel. Check for level by first cutting a scrap of wood to fit between the brackets. Place the scrap so that it spans the front end of the brackets, and rest a torpedo level on the scrap. Adjust as necessary and repeat for the back end. Check for parallel by measuring from bracket to bracket at the front and back. If the measurements aren't equal, add shims behind the end with the larger measurement.

RIGHT

To add a shelf above the unit you just installed, cut a scrap of wood to match the desired distance between the shelves and place it on top of the lower shelf unit. Then place the template on top of the scrap and mark the mounting holes with an awl. Repeat for the opposite side, then proceed as you did for the first shelf.

Install Shelves

1 **SEPARATE THE DRAWER FROM THE SLIDE BRACKETS.** Remove any doors to make shelf installation easier. Most slides used for pull-out shelves consist of two halves: One half attaches to the cabinet side, the other to the shelf. As a general rule of thumb, you'll need to separate these parts for installation. Check the directions to see if this is necessary.

2 **LOCATE & DRILL MOUNTING HOLES.** Use the template provided with the shelving unit to accurately locate the slides on opposite sides of the cabinet interior. If you're installing more than one shelf in a cabinet, start with the bottom shelf. Position the template as directed and press through the paper with an awl to mark the hole locations. Then drill holes at these locations with the recommended size drill bit.

3 **ATTACH THE SLIDES.** After drilling the holes, attach the slides to the inside faces of the cabinet. If the slides are adjustable they may require some assembly at this time—you may need to remove screws and remount them in different holes to achieve the desired width. Secure the slides to the cabinets with the screws provided. Set a torpedo level on top of each slide, and readjust if necessary.

4 **ADD THE SLIDING SHELF TO THE SLIDES.** Extend the slides and drop the shelf onto them. For the wire basket shown here, tabs on the bottom of the basket snap into openings on the slides. In most cases, there will be some kind of device to lock the parts together. Test the pull-out action and adjust the slide positions as necessary to get smooth action (see WHAT CAN GO WRONG, left).

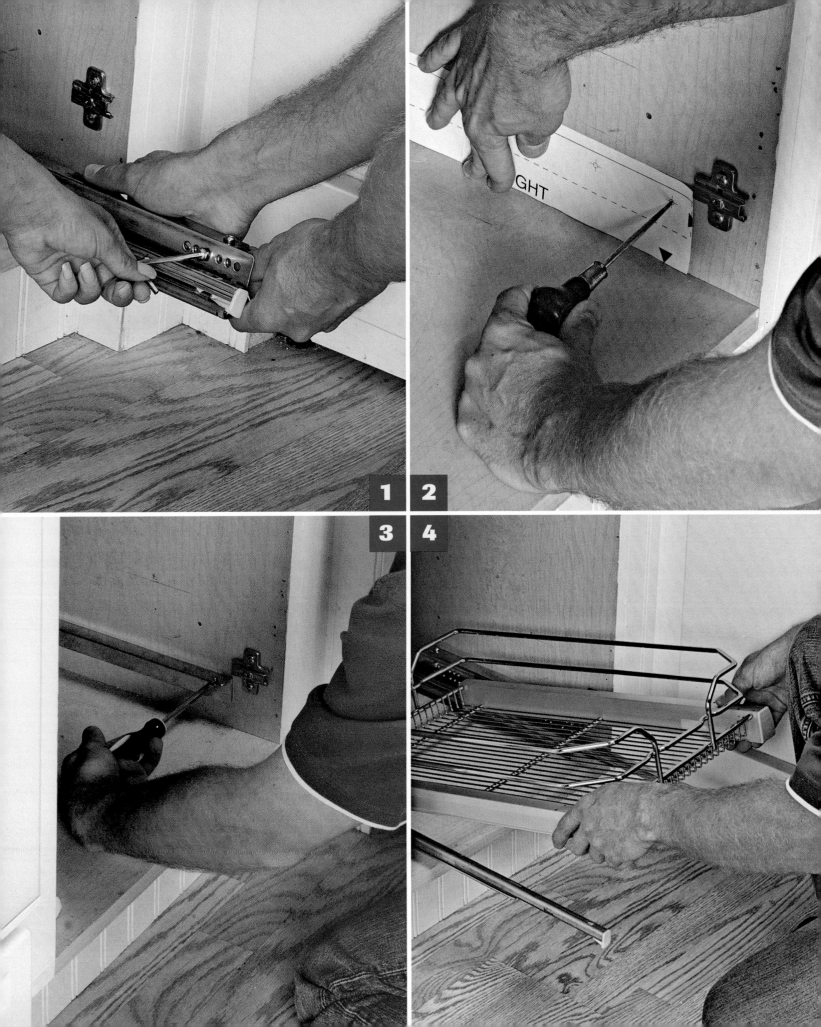

1 **2**

3 **4**

Transform a common problem—the under-counter mess of cleaning items—into an accessible, neat solution. This clever pull-out accommodates tall spray bottles, sponges, and more.

Convenience is having a trash can right where you need it, when you need it, and then tucked invisibly away when you don't.

Cabinets overflowing? Patience worn thin trying to find things? "Get organized" is easier said than done—but easy to do with accessories that help you keep things in their place and out of your way. From swivel-out pantry shelves to hide-away trash bins, space-saver organizers not only help you use the space you have, but also help make kitchen time more pleasant. Maximize your space with these ingenious helpers.

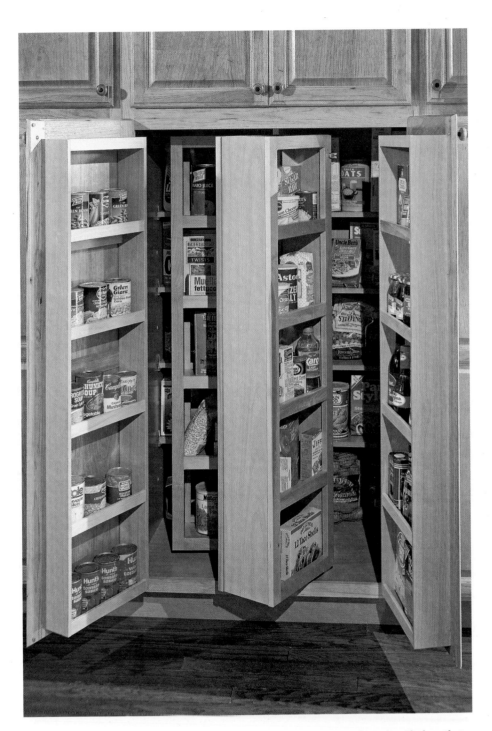

Hide-and-seek is no fun when you're searching for olive oil (or pancake mix or raisins). Stop the game with this handy center-mount pantry, which offers four easy-access tiers of storage that can be viewed from multiple sides.

Pantry shelves that just sit motionless aren't giving a full measure of service. Shelves that open out and swivel like these can easily double your storage space for food items. Since you can see almost all the contents at a glance, there's no need for the classic kitchen contortion: down on your knees, groping for something at the back of a dark shelf.

As you open the door to this corner cabinet, the half-circle wooden trays rotate out individually to give instant access to the contents.

Don't let space go to waste. This shelving unit allows for a pull-out drawer for most-often-used pots and pans. Heavy pots or those not used as frequently stay put on the bottom of the cabinet.

Unleash the storage potential of your under-sink cabinet doors to keep things neat and within reach. The shallow top shelf is ideal for scrubbing/cleaning devices, while the bottom is tall enough for bottles and boxes.

Want to double the usefulness of your utensil drawer? Try this double-decker unit. The top element slides to permit access to all the tools and kitchen gadgets underneath.

These handsome units are really multitaskers—the airflow around the wicker baskets keeps produce fresh longer, while the pull-out mechanism keeps everything out of your way until you need it.

Organization is the spice of life with this pull-out spice drawer. Tiers of slanted platforms allow for easy viewing and place your favorite seasonings right at your fingertips.

Sink & Faucet Upgrade

Transform the centerpiece of your kitchen with a new SINK & FAUCET

THIS MAKEOVER PROJECT NOT ONLY LOOKS GREAT but also makes your time in the kitchen more enjoyable. The kitchen sink and faucet are the most-used fixtures in the home, so look for replacements that suit your decor and needs. The double-bowl sink and single-handle faucet we've chosen look smart and operate smoothly. With the almost endless array of styles and finishes available today the hardest part of this upgrade will be choosing fixtures to help create the kitchen of your dreams.

REMOVE THE OLD SINK   **INSTALL THE FAUCET**   **INSERT THE NEW SINK BOWL**   **CONNECT THE PLUMBING**

✦ DO IT NOW

Before you begin any plumbing work, it's best to drain the water from the lines. If your faucet has shut-off valves, close them and open the faucet to drain out any water in the faucet. For faucets without shut-off valves, turn off the water at the main shut-off valve (usually near the water meter) and then open the sink faucet. For best results, open all faucets in your home to completely drain all the water from the lines.

✛ WHAT CAN GO WRONG

An important step in picking out a sink and faucet combo is to check that the number of holes the faucet requires matches the number of holes in the sink. Also check that the distance between the holes for the faucet match those of the sink. This will save you from the frustrating task of drilling holes into your new sink.

Tools & Gear

Many of the tools you'll need to replace a sink and faucet are probably already in your toolbox. There are also a couple of specialty tools that will help make the job easier.

ADJUSTABLE WRENCH. You'll need a wrench to tighten and loosen smaller nuts and fittings.

SLIP-JOINT PLIERS. The jaws of the pliers slide in a slot to adjust over a wide range, making them useful for tackling larger nuts and fittings.

SCREWDRIVERS & NUTDRIVER. A trusty screwdriver will remove and tighten sink-mounting clips and the screws that secure various faucet parts. Use a nutdriver for sink-mounting clips that have a bolt-type head.

STRAINER WRENCH OR NEEDLE-NOSE PLIERS. The business end of a strainer wrench is notched to fit over the X-shaped casting in the bottom of the strainer. Needle-nose pliers can also do the job.

BASIN WRENCHES. The long extension arm of a basin wrench allows you to loosen or tighten faucet-mounting nuts in the clear space below a sink. The serrated jaws on the end are self-adjusting—they close to fit around the nut as pressure is applied.

SOCKET SETS. A set of ratchets and incremental-sized sockets make quick work of loosening and tightening various nuts and bolts.

PUTTY KNIVES. Both the plastic and metal varieties will come in handy to break old sealant bonds between sinks and countertops and to remove old sealant residue.

RAGS, BUCKET & GLOVES. Plug up the open end of the waste line with rags, and use a bucket to catch water from the supply lines. Wear work gloves to protect your hands when lifting out your old sink.

WHAT'S DIFFERENT?

Pipes can be joined together with either permanent or temporary fittings. Permanent fittings for copper pipe are soldered, or "sweated," together. The fitting is heated with a propane torch until it's hot enough to melt solder. Solder is flowed into the joint to create a strong, watertight seal. Temporary fittings are used in places that periodically need maintenance or replacement—such as lines and valves to fixtures like faucets. The most common temporary fitting is a compression fitting, which has three parts: a fitting, or body; a ferrule, or compression ring; and a compression nut. The nut and ferrule slip over the pipe, which is inserted into the fitting. Tightening the nut compresses the ferrule into the fitting, creating a watertight joint.

What to Buy

1| SINK. Before you go sink shopping, measure the width and depth of your current sink—you don't want one that doesn't match the opening in your countertop. Unless you want to replumb the waste lines, you should pick a sink that has a similar bowl size and configuration. You'll also need to be aware of the different ways sinks attach to countertops (see SINK-MOUNTING OPTIONS, below). Finally, pick a sink with the same number of holes required for mounting the faucet—a good reason to pick your faucet first.

2| FAUCET. First decide if you want one or two handles. Then look at sprayer options—choose from a separate sprayer, a pull-out sprayer, or none at all. You'll also have choices in mountings: Some faucets mount in a single hole in the sink, but many require three. Finally, pick a style that blends with the other elements in your kitchen.

3| FLEXIBLE SUPPLY LINES. The simplest way to connect a new faucet to existing supply lines is with flexible supply lines—available wherever plumbing supplies are sold.

4| SINK TRAP KIT. If your new sink has the same bowl configuration as your old one, you may be able to use your existing trap and waste fittings (the pipes underneath the sink). Otherwise, you'll need a new plastic sink trap kit to hook up the sink. You may also need extension tubes that run between the strainers and the trap fittings.

5| TEFLON TAPE & PLUMBER'S PUTTY. Virtually every plumbing project you tackle will need some type of sealant to prevent leaks. When you shop for your fittings, make sure to pick up some Teflon tape and plumber's putty.

SINK-MOUNTING OPTIONS

Forming a watertight seal between the countertop and sink is critical when mounting a sink. Here are the five most common mounting methods.

1| DROP-IN OR SELF-RIMMING. A true self-rimming or porcelain cast-iron sink relies on its significant weight and a thin layer of sealant to create a seal. When set in place, the weight of the sink squeezes out any excess sealant, forming a watertight seal under the small flat on the rim.

2| SELF-RIMMING WITH CLIPS. Although called self-rimming, this style of sink (the common stainless-steel kitchen variety) really isn't. A dozen or so clips hook onto a lip on the underside of the sink and pull the sink tight against the countertop as the screws are tightened.

3| FLUSH WITH TILE. For kitchens with a tile countertop, the sink is usually installed first and then the tile is added. The disadvantage here is that the grout surrounding the sink will allow water to seep in, eventually causing the seal between the sink and countertop to fail.

4| UNDER-COUNTER. Under-counter sinks are pressed up under a solid-surface countertop and held in place with clips that screw into inserts embedded in the countertop. Silicone caulk is used as a sealant and also serves as an adhesive that helps hold the sink in place.

5| INTEGRAL SINK/COUNTERTOP. Forming the sink and the countertop out of the same material and gluing them together is the best way to keep water from seeping between them.

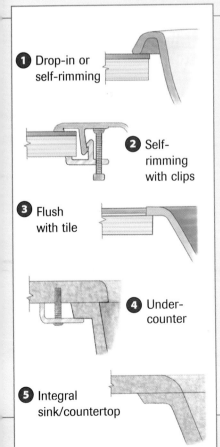

1 Drop-in or self-rimming
2 Self-rimming with clips
3 Flush with tile
4 Under-counter
5 Integral sink/countertop

Out with the Old…

1 **REMOVE THE DOORS FOR BETTER ACCESS.** Since the space under a sink is tight, remove the doors from the sink base cabinet. This way, you won't be constantly bumping into them as you work.

2 **DISCONNECT THE SUPPLY & WASTE LINES.** Turn off the water supply to the faucet (see DO IT NOW, p. 52). Open the faucet to drain out any water in the pipes. Then use an adjustable wrench to loosen the coupling nuts that connect the supply lines to the faucet—

have a bucket underneath to catch any water in the lines. Next, loosen the slip nuts that connect the trap to the tailpiece and waste line. Then carefully remove the trap and empty it into the bucket, and remove the supply and waste lines.

3 **REMOVE THE SINK-MOUNTING CLIPS.** Working from underneath the sink, remove any mounting clips, if applicable. Use a screwdriver or nutdriver to loosen the clips, and then disengage them from the sink with your fingers.

4 **LIFT OUT THE OLD SINK.** Before you lift out the sink, break any existing putty bonds with a putty knife (see DO IT RIGHT, left). Put on a pair of gloves to protect your hands from sharp metal edges, then gently push the sink up from the bottom. As soon as you have enough room, slip your fingers under the lip of the sink and lift it out. If your old sink is cast iron, insert "finger-saver" blocks (thin scraps of lumber or shims) under the rim to prevent the weight of the sink from crushing your fingers. Also, have a partner help lift out and set aside the old sink—cast iron is heavy.

5 **CLEAN UP THE COUNTERTOP.** With the old sink out, use a plastic putty knife to scrape off any sealant residue. If you must use a metal putty knife, wrap a clean cloth over the end to help prevent the knife edge from scratching your countertop.

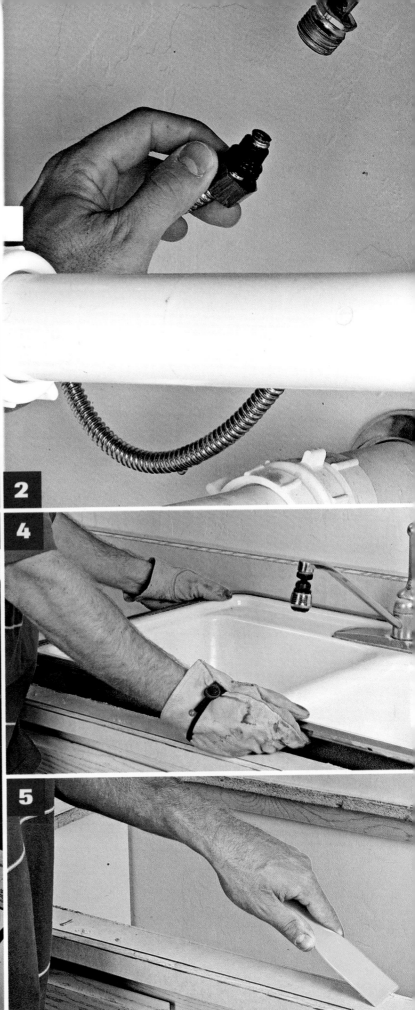

1 **2**
3 **4**
5

◆ DO IT NOW

Chrome and other finished faucet parts can be easily scratched by most pliers. To prevent this, wrap masking or duct tape around the jaws of your pliers before using them on these delicate parts.

➕ WHAT CAN GO WRONG

Check for leaks inside the base cabinet by feeling along the plumbing lines. If you feel any water seepage, find the source. Then turn off the water, retighten the connection, and check again. If necessary, disassemble the leaky joint (for supply lines), reapply Teflon tape, and reconnect. For waste lines, tighten joints and replace the washer if necessary.

...In with the New

6 **INSTALL THE FAUCET.** Install the faucet in the sink before you install the whole unit—you'll have better access to the mounting nuts. Place a towel or drop cloth on the countertop. Turn the sink upside down and slide it over on the countertop so it overhangs far enough to let you insert the faucet from underneath. Use the gasket supplied to secure the faucet and tighten the mounting nuts with a screwdriver.

7 **INSTALL THE STRAINER.** Install the strainer before setting the sink in place. Squeeze out a generous coil of plumber's putty and wrap it around the inside edge of the strainer. Then follow the manufacturer's directions for gasket placement and insert the strainer into the basin hole. Thread on the nut and then tighten the strainer by inserting a pair of needle-nose pliers or a strainer wrench in the bottom of the strainer. You'll get a lot of putty squeezing out as you twist to tighten. Remove the excess and wipe away any putty residue with a clean cloth.

8 **CREATE A SEAL.** Self-rimming sinks rely on a sealant to keep water on the countertop from seeping under the rim. Apply a continuous 1/2-in.-diameter coil of plumber's putty or a generous bead of silicone caulk around the rim. Alternately, you can apply the sealant to the edge of the sink cutout.

9 **INSERT & SECURE THE SINK.** Lift up the sink, turn it over, and set it into the sink opening. It should be a snug fit. Press down to squeeze out any excess putty or caulk. Clean up the excess later after tightening the mounting clips, if applicable. If you are using clips, space them out equally on all sides and then tighten them in the sequence recommended by the manufacturer, using a screwdriver or nutdriver.

10 **RECONNECT & TEST THE LINES.** Reconnect the supply lines to the faucet and sink first, and then connect the waste lines. Before turning on the water, remove the faucet aerator to keep it from clogging with impurities in the system. When the water looks clean, reattach the aerator. If you've installed a pull-out sprayer, attach the counterweight to the sprayer hose so it will retract into the faucet when not in use.

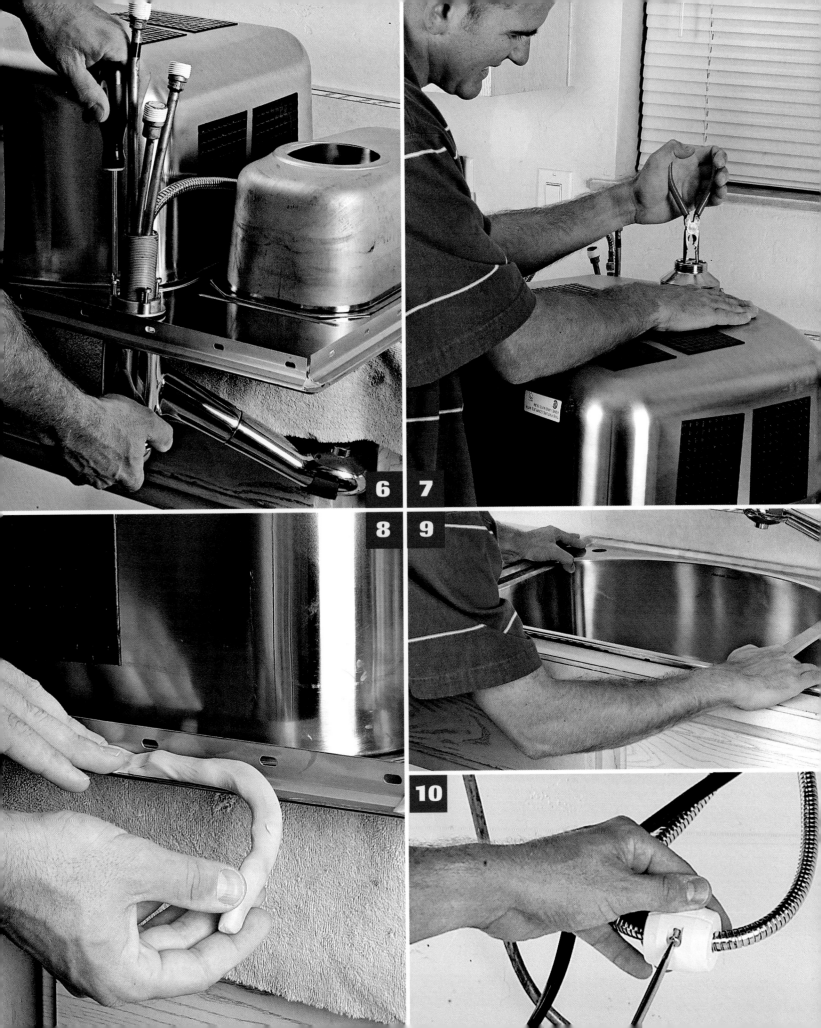

6 7

8 9

10

For cooking and cleanup, this double-bowl, front-apron model does double duty because the bowls are about the same size. Recessed tiles at the front add charm to the solid-surface material that cleans like a dream.

A perennial favorite, gleaming stainless steel pleases both the eyes and ears. The sound-deadening feature of this single-bowl model cuts down on noise when the water is turned on.

Time to throw in the (dish) towel on the old kitchen sink? Let the most-used plumbing fixture in the house reflect your style with today's abundance of designs. Whether one or two bowls, stainless steel or solid-surface, contemporary or country, today's sinks turn on a gleaming array of good looks and efficient performance.

You'll be surprised at the number of colors available for porcelain sinks. From loganberry to bone to rhapsody blue (shown below) there's a hue for every mood.

Glossy porcelain over lightweight steel puts a fresh finish on this dual-level sink. Wash pots in the deep side, rinse carrots in the other, and enjoy the versatility for years.

For a country kitchen, here's the perfect country sink in vitreous china. From the high backsplash to the distinctive profile, it brings old-fashioned form to 21st-century function.

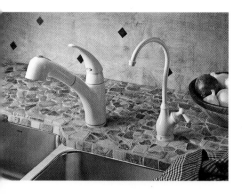

This simple ivory-toned faucet offers a nice contrast to the tile mosaic. Many faucet models come with an accompanying water filter.

Today's waterworks
pour on the choices: chrome, bronze, or brushed nickel finish; single or double handle; pull-out or deck-mounted sprayer. And don't forget about the soap dispenser. With so many styles to choose from, you're sure to find something that complements your kitchen decor and provides the function you need.

The gooseneck swoop of this faucet frees up working space under the water flow. The deck-mounted handle, soap dispenser, and sprayer place everything you need right at hand.

Like things simple and sleek? Consider this faucet with a gooseneck shape for accessibility, a pull-out sprayer for ease, a single-handle lever, and a soap dispenser.

Here's a new twist on a classic style. The upward arch keeps the faucet clear of working hands, while the sprayer stands aside until needed.

A bold bronze finish and intriguing Victorian styling make a strong design statement. Fixtures this stylish take center stage when installed in a simple sink.

Lighting Solutions

Add BRIGHTNESS AND STYLE with new fixtures overhead and under your cabinets

DOES MOST OF THE LIGHT IN YOUR KITCHEN come from a single overhead fixture, with a bit of daylight from one window trickling in to illuminate the sink? This setup leaves you working in the dark—literally. The food prep areas—namely, your counters and stovetop—call for ample lighting to allow for safe use of sharp knives, hot pans, and scalding liquids. Fortunately, installing new overhead and under-cabinet lighting is fairly simple. With a few tools and a little time, you can get illuminating results.

REMOVE OLD FIXTURE   INSTALL MOUNTING PLATE   WIRE THE NEW FIXTURE   MOUNT THE NEW FIXTUR

▸▪ LINGO

Some areas in the kitchen may not need an entire strip of lights. Here's where small, individual, hockey puck–shaped halogen lights are ideal. Puck lights are available in packs of two or more and can be mounted exactly where you need the light.

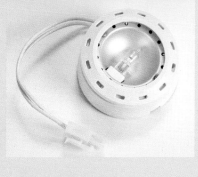

▶ DO IT RIGHT

To prevent someone in your home from inadvertently turning on power to a circuit you're working on, place a piece of masking tape labeled "No!" across the breaker you've flipped or the fuse you've removed. This will alert others that work is in progress and prevent any shocking situations.

Tools & Gear

Installing or upgrading the lighting in your kitchen is one of the least tool-intensive makeover projects you can tackle. You probably own many of the tools listed below.

TAPE MEASURE. You'll need a tape measure to make sure your installed under-cabinet lights are centered and the same distance out from the wall.

SCREWDRIVERS. You'll need a screwdriver for fastening the screws for under-cabinet lighting. (The screws are too small for a drill/driver.) Removing and installing new overhead fixtures is also easier with a screwdriver, which is less cumbersome than a drill/driver.

DRILL & BITS. Whether or not you need a drill depends on the size of the screws used to hold under-cabinet lighting in place. In many cases, the screws are so small that you can simply create a starter hole with an awl and drive the screws right in.

AWL. An awl is the perfect tool for marking screw-mounting locations for under-cabinet lighting. If you're working with strip lighting that comes with a paper template for locating mounting screws, you can position the template and press through the paper to mark hole locations on the cabinet bottom. For hard or dense cabinets, you may need to tap the handle of the awl with a hammer to make a mark deep enough to be easily seen.

WIRE STRIPPERS. Since most new fixtures come with the wires prestripped, you may not need wire strippers. Still, a stripper is useful for cleaning up existing wiring that you'll use to connect to your new light fixture.

LINESMAN PLIERS. These specialty pliers, sometimes referred to as electrician's pliers, combine the cutting power of diagonal cutters with the gripping ability of slip-joint pliers. They're the perfect tool for cutting, twisting, and manipulating wires.

CIRCUIT TESTER. A circuit tester provides a quick and inexpensive way to safely check for power. Simply touch the two leads to the fixture wires—if the light glows, you have power.

SAFETY 101

Here's a refresher course in electric safety. Always shut off power before working on an electrical project. Whenever possible, reach into a circuit with only one hand. Using both hands puts your heart in the direct path of the current in case of an electrical short. Wear rubber-soled shoes and never work alone. Use a nonconducting fiberglass ladder instead of the conductive metal variety.

What to Buy

To make over your kitchen lighting, you'll need a new overhead fixture and some form of under-cabinet lighting. Whichever type you buy, check the packaging to see if light bulbs are included.

1| UNDER-CABINET LIGHTING. There are many types and sizes of under-cabinet lighting: individual pucks, strips of pucks, strip fluorescents, and even flexible light strips. Individual pucks have the most flexibility, as they allow you to position the lights exactly where you need them. The downside is that they're more complicated to install and wire than a simple strip light. Strip lights go up quickly and offer plenty of light, but your lighting locations are limited. The type of lights you pick—halogen or fluorescent—depends on your lighting preferences. Halogen lights produce a more natural light than fluorescents but generate quite a bit of heat; fluorescents run very cool.

2| OVERHEAD LIGHTING. Choices of overhead lighting range from simple, low-profile recessed lights to multisegment pendants. Low-profile "cans," such as spotlights, are quick and easy to install but tend to light only a small portion of the kitchen. Pendant lights suspended from the ceiling via metal tubes bring the light closer to worksurfaces. Multisegment pendants spread the light over a wider area and are the lighting of choice for placement over kitchen islands. One thing to keep in mind when shopping for a new light fixture is its weight. The existing electrical box may not be strong enough to handle a heavy fixture. In cases like this, you'll need to either select a lighter fixture or upgrade to a box that's capable of bearing the weight. (See WHAT CAN GO WRONG, p. 68, for more on these special boxes.)

3| LIGHT BULBS. Virtually all under-cabinet lights come with bulbs included—and already installed. If you're installing halogen lights, take care not to handle the bulbs. These delicate lamps tend to burn out prematurely if they come in contact with skin oil. Overhead lights generally do not come with bulbs, so check the box label for type and recommended size.

4| WIRE NUTS (OPTIONAL). Most new lighting comes with the wire nuts you'll need to make your electrical connections (see COOL TOOL, below). But you should have a variety of sizes on hand in case you need a larger or smaller wire nut than those supplied with the fixture.

COOL TOOL

Wire nuts are used to quickly connect wires and are color-coded so you'll know how many wires you can safely splice together. The most common are yellow and red: yellow can splice three 12-gauge wires or four 14-gauge wires; red can handle three 10-gauge, four 12-gauge, or five 14-gauge wires. Quality wire nuts house a square-cut spring that cuts into and grips the wires as the nut is twisted into place.

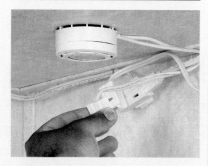

Connecting multiple puck lights with under-cabinet wiring is simple: A two-part plug snaps onto the end of each light. These plugs are then inserted in a short extension cord provided with the light. Plug this cord in and flip on the switch for bright countertops.

Many kitchen cabinets have only a shallow recess in their bottoms to accept under-cabinet lighting. This means the lighting can actually protrude and be visible. You can hide the lights by attaching a decorative strip of molding to the bottom front edge of the cabinets.

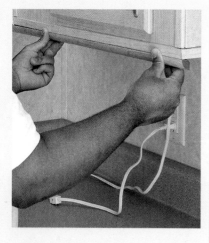

Under-Cabinet Lighting

1 **LOCATE THE BEST POSITION.** Though most manufacturers suggest locating lights as close to the front of the cabinet as possible to give the best coverage, you may find that you like the light farther back. The best way to determine which position works best for you is to plug in a light and hold it under the cabinet so you can see how it illuminates the worksurface in various places. Mark the spot that works best for you.

2 **MARK MOUNTING HOLES.** Once you've located the ideal position for each light, use the template provided or the light itself and an awl to mark the holes for the mounting hardware. Tape the template in place or hold the light and press the awl into the underside of the cabinet at each hole. If the mounting screws are small, you may not need to drill pilot holes. If you do, check the manufacturer's instructions for the recommended-size drill bit and drill holes at each location.

3 **INSTALL THE LIGHT.** To install each light, simply drive the screws through the lights and into the punched or drilled hole locations. Take care not to overtighten these—you're typically only driving into 1/4-in.- to 1/2-in.-thick wood, and the screws can easily strip out.

4 **ASSEMBLE THE LIGHT (IF APPLICABLE).** Most puck lights have a base that attaches to the underside of the cabinet and a lens that snaps onto the base. Align the tabs in the lens with those in the base and press into position. In most cases, you'll need to rotate the lens to lock it in place.

5 **WIRE IT UP.** If you've installed strip lighting, just plug it in and turn it on. Individual halogen pucks require a bit more work. Route the wires from each light to a common location, usually near an electrical receptacle. Use self-adhesive clips to hold wires in place. Assemble the plugs on the ends of each lamp wire—typically two-part plugs that press together over the wire to make a connection. Connect each of the plugs to the extension cord provided and plug it in.

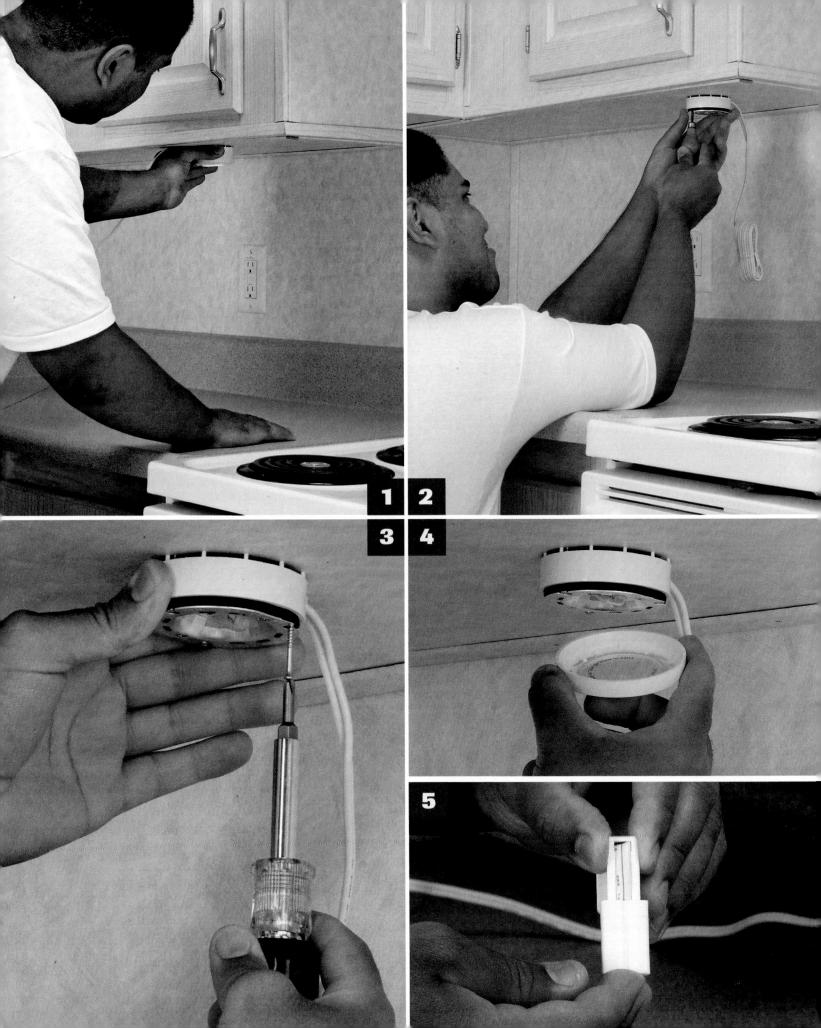

Overhead fixtures can be heavy and are often hard to support with one hand while you try to connect the wires with the other. The solution? Bend a wire coat hanger into an S-shape, then hook one end onto the electrical box and hang the fixture on the other end. This leaves both hands free for wiring.

+ WHAT CAN GO WRONG

Fixtures that weigh less than 50 lbs. can usually be supported by most electrical boxes (assuming they were installed correctly). But if the new fixture weighs more than 50 lbs., code requires that you install a heavy-duty electrical box that attaches to the ceiling joists to better support the fixture. These special boxes attach to metal brackets that fit between and attach to your ceiling joists.

Overhead Lighting

1 **REMOVE THE OLD FIXTURE.** Begin by turning off the power to the fixture and tagging the panel to avoid an accident (see DO IT RIGHT, p. 64). Then remove the glass globe or diffuser and the light bulb(s). Next, unscrew the retaining nut that holds the decorative cover plate onto the electrical box. Before you disconnect the wires, double-check to make sure the power is off with a circuit tester. Then unscrew the wire nuts, separate the wires, and set the old fixture aside.

2 **ATTACH THE NEW MOUNTING STRAP.** In homes built before 1959, incandescent light fixtures were often mounted directly to an electrical box. Code now requires that the fixture be mounted to a flat metal bar called a mounting strap that is secured to the box. Most new fixtures include a mounting strap, or you can buy a "universal" mounting strap at your local hardware store. Fasten the strap to the box with the screws provided.

3 **WIRE THE NEW FIXTURE.** Before you install the new fixture, take a look at the wires coming out of the electrical box. If the insulation is cracked or the ends are nicked, tarnished, or corroded, use a wire stripper to cut the ends off and strip off ½ in. of insulation. Next, follow the manufacturer's instructions on how to attach the new fixture wires to the circuit wires with the wire nuts that are supplied with the new fixture.

4 **ATTACH THE NEW FIXTURE TO THE MOUNTING STRAP.** Finally, attach the fixture to the mounting strap with the screws or nuts provided. Then add the bulbs or diffusers (if applicable). Diffusers are commonly held in place with decorative caps or retaining nuts. Tighten these friction-tight and no more—overtightening can crack the diffuser.

1 **2**
3 **4**

A pair of Arts and Crafts–style mini–pendants illuminate the counter/seating area while blending with the room's decor. The weathered bronze finish and art glass complement the color used in the kitchen.

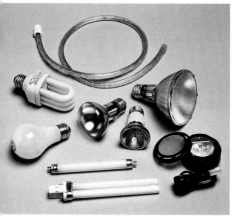

Let's get down to bulb basics. Lighten up with familiar incandescents in bulb or rope form; try brighter, longer-lasting halogens in pucks or reflectors; or use fluorescents in twin- or triple-tube versions.

Are you in the dark about kitchen lighting? Brighten up your space with versatile overhead lights, and illuminate your work area with under-cabinet fixtures. You can literally spotlight the room's best features—while casting a kind shadow on less-desirable aspects—just by choosing the right light. It's all just an "On" switch away.

This fluorescent fixture has a sleek, simple design and hangs just 6 in. from the ceiling, making it a good choice for just about any decor.

Showcase your beautiful crossbeams, gleaming cookware, or other distinctive elements with "cans," or spotlights, placed to focus on your feature of choice.

Prepare, eat, and clean up, all under the activity-specific light of simple pendant fixtures. Each light is set to a custom height by simply adjusting the length of the chains.

Hung above the island cooktop and sink, handblown Deco pendants with satin aluminum caps jazz up a traditional kitchen.

Shed a generous amount of light on your counter workspace with basic under-cabinet fluorescent tubes.

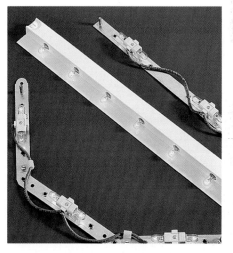

To cast a subtle glow at night or to light up a counter workspace anytime, these strips of mini-lights are a great choice.

Want overhead lighting that *really* sets you apart? There's an almost endless array of fun, funky shapes and styles available—from low-hanging pendants to space-age track lighting.

Cookbook Shelf

Keep cookbooks and curios close at hand with an **ELEGANT SHELF** you can make from stock lumber and molding

I F YOU'RE LOOKING FOR A PLACE to keep your cookbooks handy, it's hard to top this easy-to-build shelf. You simply screw together the components (made from any solid wood), then stain or paint the shelf to accent your kitchen decor. The moldings serve double duty: They're a graceful accent and also hide the assembly screws. You can easily modify this simple design to suit your own needs; maybe you'll find you really need more than one. Caution: Once friends and family spot this nifty shelf, you'll be asked to make another, and another...

| CUT OUT THE PARTS | ASSEMBLE THE SHELF | APPLY A FINISH | HANG IT AND ENJOY |

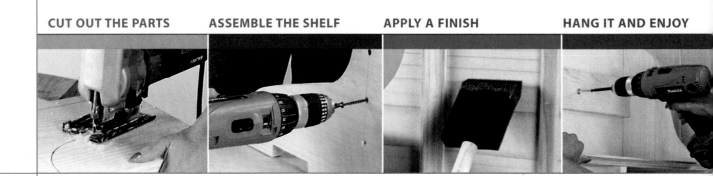

When choosing the right blade for your saber saw bear in mind that more teeth per inch affords a smoother cut, but the cutting is slower. In general, blades with 7 to 14 teeth per inch will cut most woods just fine. Most blades are made from high-speed steel (HSS) and are fine for general-purpose work. Scroll-cut blades have narrower bodies and finer teeth for smooth cuts in tight turns in wood.

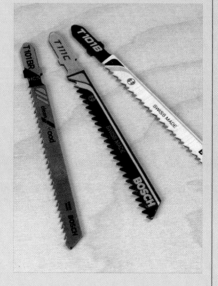

■ LINGO

Commonly used in home construction, a ledger is any horizontal piece of wood used as a shelf-like support for lumber that butts up against or rests on top of the horizontal piece. For our cookbook shelf, the ledger sits in the recess between the top and bottom shelves.

Tools & Gear

If you've ever done any carpentry or trim work on your home, you probably have most of the tools listed below. If you don't have some of the power tools, consider renting or borrowing them from a friend.

TAPE MEASURE. A quality 12-ft. tape measure is essential for measuring boards to length and laying out the side profiles.

CORDLESS DRILL/DRIVER & BITS. A drill/driver beats a regular drill in this case since it can drill holes and drive the screws that hold the shelf together. A small eight-piece set of drill bits is plenty for this project.

SCREWDRIVER. If you don't have access to a drill/driver, you'll need a screwdriver to assemble the shelf.

COMBINATION SQUARE. This is really four measuring and layout tools in one: a metal rule, a try square, a miter square, and a depth gauge. This tool makes laying out right angles a snap.

SABER SAW. This is the tool of choice for making curved cuts. With its thin blades and powerful motor, it can handle complex cuts with ease.

HANDSAW & MITER BOX. In order for wood parts to butt cleanly up against each other, the ends need to be cut perfectly square. Here's where a miter box shines. A slot in the miter box accepts a handsaw and guides it to make straight cuts.

HAMMER & NAIL SET. The moldings of the cookbook shelf are attached with glue and nails. After you've driven the nails in close to the surface of the molding, stop and drive them slightly below the surface with a nail set.

PUTTY KNIFE. You can use your finger to fill nail holes with putty, but you'll get better results with a putty knife.

STUD FINDER & TORPEDO LEVEL. You'll need to mount the shelf to wall studs. A stud finder will help you locate them. Use a level to ensure that the ledger hangs correctly.

FOAM BRUSH. Regardless of the finish you choose, a 2-in. foam brush is a quick and inexpensive way to apply the finish.

DOUBLE-SIDED TAPE. Using double-sided tape to hold the two shelf sides together as you cut out the shape will guarantee identical profiles.

CLAMPS. Although not absolutely essential, a couple of bar clamps can hold the parts of the shelf together as you drive in screws. You'll need clamps that can span at least 26 in.

What to Buy

1| LUMBER. Pine, poplar, and red oak are all good choices for your cookbook shelf and can be found at most home centers and lumber yards. Pine is soft, light, and relatively inexpensive. Poplar, although light, is a hardwood and works well with hand tools. Its only downside is that it can have yellow, green, and black shades of grain on a single board. This makes it an excellent choice for a painted shelf. Red oak is hard, heavy, beautiful, and expensive. A shelf made from red oak can weigh three times as much as one made from pine. Oak is also much harder to work with than either pine or poplar.

2| MOLDING. The cookbook shelf shown here uses two different kinds of molding to hide the assembly screws. We used 3/4-in. by 3/4-in. cove molding for the top shelf and 3/4-in. screen molding for the bottom shelf. You can use any type you like as long as it hides the screws. Also, you can dress up the shelf by adding a length of crown molding under the bottom shelf as shown on p. 82.

3| SCREWS & NAILS. You'll need about a dozen each of 2-in. and 1⅝-in. drywall screws. The longer 2-in. screws are used to attach the sides to the shelves. The extra length helps provide a strong grip in the end grain of the shelves. The 1⅝-in. screws are used to attach the divider and the back rail. You'll also need a box of 1-in.-long brads for attaching the molding.

4| SANDPAPER. A couple of sheets of 150-grit open-coat sandpaper will smooth out any imperfections in the shelf. If you're after a super-smooth finish, sand again with 220-grit sandpaper.

5| PAINT & FINISH. If you want the natural beauty of the wood to show, apply a couple of coats of polyurethane—enhance the grain by staining it before applying a top coat. Alternately, you can paint the shelf to match your cabinets or choose a different color to serve as an accent. Whatever paint you choose, it's best to apply a sealer or primer first, especially if you used pine: The knots can bleed sap right through the paint if not sealed properly.

6| MATCHING PUTTY. For shelves finished with a clear top coat, choose a matching putty to fill the nail holes. It's best to pick a matching putty after you apply the finish. Look for crayon-like wax putty sticks wherever paint is sold. If you're painting the shelf, any putty that hardens will do. Don't use the wax-stick variety here—it doesn't harden and will not accept paint.

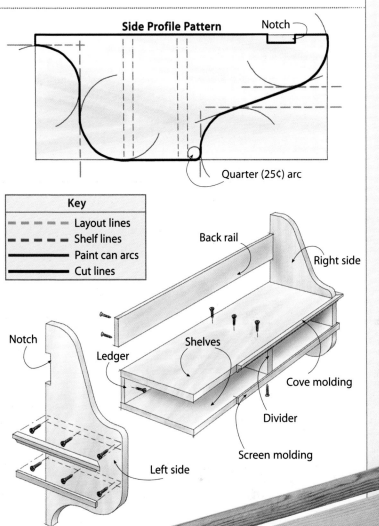

COOKBOOK SHELF DIAGRAM

Side Profile Pattern | Notch

Quarter (25¢) arc

Key	
– – –	Layout lines
— — —	Shelf lines
——	Paint can arcs
▬▬▬	Cut lines

Back rail

Right side

Notch

Ledger

Shelves

Cove molding

Divider

Screen molding

Left side

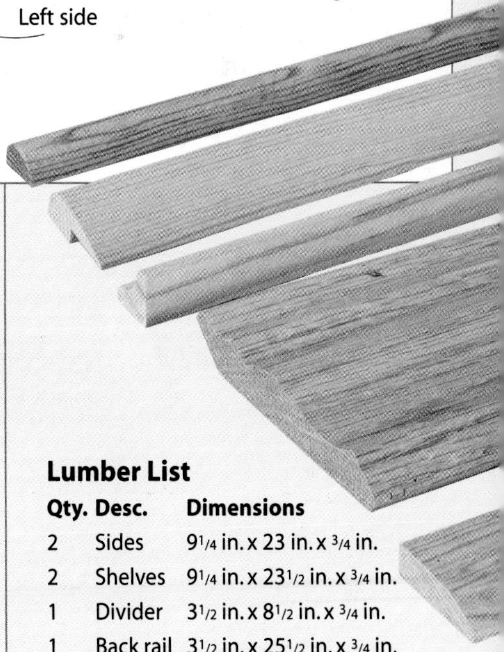

Lumber List

Qty.	Desc.	Dimensions
2	Sides	9¼ in. x 23 in. x ¾ in.
2	Shelves	9¼ in. x 23½ in. x ¾ in.
1	Divider	3½ in. x 8½ in. x ¾ in.
1	Back rail	3½ in. x 25½ in. x ¾ in.
1	Ledger	3½ in. x 23½ in. x ¾ in.
Cove & screen molding		cut to fit

Lay Out, Cut & Assemble

1 **LAY OUT THE SIDE PROFILE.** To build the cookbook shelf, start by cutting the sides to length (see LUMBER LIST, p. 77). You'll only need to lay out one side profile. Start by drawing five layout lines as shown on the pattern on p. 77. Next, using a 1-gallon paint can as a template,  draw four arcs as shown on the pattern. Use a quarter (25¢ piece) to draw the small arc in the top corner of the front. Connect the arcs as shown with a pencil and a straightedge. Finally, lay out the notch for the back rail. It's 3 in. down from the top back edge and is 3/4 in. wide by 3 1/2 in. long.

 **2** **CUT OUT THE SIDES.** With the side profile laid out, you can cut out the shape with a saber saw. The easiest way to get matching side profiles is to temporarily tape the sides together, place them on a worksurface, and then cut the profiles for both sides at the same time. A couple of 12-in.-long lengthwise strips of double-sided tape will hold the sides together just fine. To keep the base of the saber saw from scratching the wood—especially if you're using pine—apply masking tape to the bottom of the saw's base before cutting out the profile.

3 **CUT THE REMAINING PARTS TO LENGTH.** With the sides complete, you can turn your attention to the remaining parts. Consult the LUMBER LIST on p. 77 and cut the remaining parts to length—except for the molding. These pieces are cut to fit around the assembled shelf.

4 **ASSEMBLE THE SHELF.** Lay out the three screw locations on both the top and bottom shelves for the center divider. The middle screws are centered, and the outer screws are 1 in. in from the ends. Drill pilot holes for the screws, and then screw the shelves to the divider with their front edges flush. You'll notice a 3/4-in. recess in the back—this is to make room for the ledger, which you'll add later. Lay out screw locations on the sides (four screws per shelf on both sides) and screw the sides to the shelves. Here's where bar clamps come in handy.

1

2

3

4

Don't rely solely on eyesight to level this handsome shelf. Instead, use a torpedo level and mark the ledger location with a pencil.

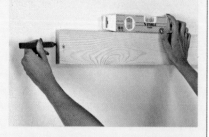

✛ WHAT CAN GO WRONG

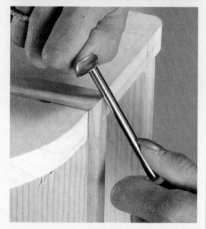

Even if you've mitered carefully, the joint where mitered moldings meet can end up with a gap. Close the gap by pressing the smooth shank of a screwdriver against the joint to compress or "burnish" the gap closed.

Finishing Touches

5 **ADD THE MOLDING.** Once the shelf is assembled, you can cut and attach the molding to conceal the assembly screws. Start by measuring one side and cutting a piece to length. The back edge is cut straight, and the front edge is cut at 45 degrees. Using a miter box and handsaw will make it easier to cut the ends square. Measure and cut the next piece, continuing in this same manner until you've wrapped both sets of molding around the sides and shelves. When done, set the brads below the surface with a nail set and fill the holes with putty. If you're not painting the shelf, hold off on the putty until the finish has been applied.

6 **FINISH THE SHELF.** Sand the completed shelf with 150-grit sandpaper, vacuum or brush off any dust, and set the shelf on a covered worksurface. Then apply the finish of your choice. Don't forget to apply finish to the ledger as well.

7 **LOCATE WALL STUDS.** After the finish has dried overnight, you can mount the shelf. To do this, start by locating two studs in the wall where the shelf will be mounted. An electronic stud finder makes quick work of this task. As you locate the studs, make light pencil marks on the wall indicating the stud locations.

8 **HANG THE LEDGER.** The cookbook shelf is supported in two ways: It fits over a ledger attached to the wall studs, and then the back rail is screwed into the studs. Once you've located the wall studs, hold the shelf against the wall in the desired location and have a helper mark the spot on the wall where you want the ledger to sit. Position the ledger on the wall, level it, and secure it to the wall studs by driving in a couple of 3½-in. screws with a drill/driver.

9 **HANG THE SHELF.** All that's left is to set the top shelf on the ledger and drive a couple of 3½-in. screws through the top rail into the wall studs you marked earlier.

5

6

7

8

9

Adding two flats to the side profile creates a classic ogee-like shape. This profile requires advanced layout skills. You'll need to enlarge the pattern as shown to fit a 23-in.-long 1x10. After that, the shelf construction is pretty much the same. We also added a short length of crown molding between the sides under the bottom shelf as a decorative accent. Finally, we painted the shelf a cheerful burnt orange to really make it stand out.

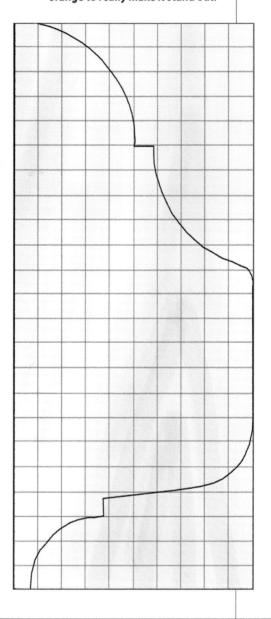

Book shelf? Cook shelf!

Who wouldn't want a handsome, handy shelf for storing cookbooks, collectibles, keys, mail, or knickknacks? You can style and paint this versatile shelf to suit your needs and your decorating theme—whether it's over the countertop or next to the door. And it's so easy to build, you'll want to make two.

One of the best things about our cookbook shelf is that it looks great in just about any color. Choose a hue that matches your kitchen decor or select something bold that shouts "look at me!"

Using quality lumber will enable you to choose from a variety of finishing options (from top): walnut, oak, unfinished, cherry, and mahogany.

Located near an entry door, this attractive oak cookbook shelf also serves as a handy organizer for both mail and keys. We used the simple profile for this shelf and built it using red oak lumber and molding. The natural beauty of the wood shows clearly through the two coats of satin polyurethane.

Consider adding a strip of corkboard to your cookbook shelf. It's perfect for keeping coupons handy and posting shopping and "to do" lists.

Cabinet Refacing

REFACE your cabinets and **REPLACE** doors and drawer fronts for a new kitchen without the cost of new cabinets

F YOUR KITCHEN CABINETS work fine but look tired, don't replace them—reface them! With roll-on self-stick veneer on the cabinets and new doors and drawer fronts to match, you'll put a fresh face on old cabinets in short order. Add new knobs and pulls to complete the transformation. It's a major makeover project that won't break your bank. All you need for a new-look kitchen is a steady hand, a little patience, and modest carpentry skills.

COVER THE ENDS   APPLY THE VENEER   ADD NEW DRAWER FRONTS   MOUNT THE NEW DOORS

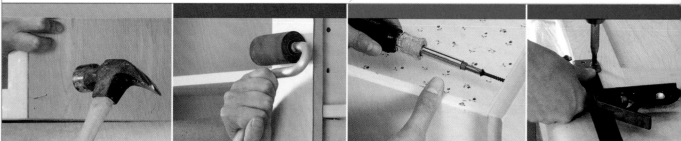

Tools & Gear

Basic carpentry tools are all you need to reface your cabinets. Specialty tools, like the laminate trimmer, will make the job easier.

TAPE MEASURE. Refacing requires accurate measuring—not only to order parts but also to lay out the veneer for cutting, marking trim for cuts, and mounting doors, drawers, and hardware.

COMBINATION SQUARE. You'll use this four-in-one tool along with a utility knife to cut perfect joints where veneer strips meet.

BLOCK PLANE. The low-angle blade on this plane makes it easy to trim end panels and veneer without worrying about grain direction.

HAMMER & NAIL SET. End panels and trim are attached with brads and a hammer. Use a nail set to drive brads below the surface so you can add putty to hide the holes.

SCISSORS & UTILITY KNIFE. You can cut self-stick veneer with ordinary scissors, and it's easy to trim to size with a utility knife. Make sure you have sharp blades handy.

PRYBAR. If your old drawer fronts are nailed to the false fronts, a prybar will separate them.

SCREWDRIVER OR CORDLESS DRILL/DRIVER. You can attach drawer fronts, doors, and hardware with a screwdriver or a drill/driver fitted with a screwdriver bit. With the amount of assembly required for the average kitchen, the drill/driver is your best bet.

DRILL & BITS. If you don't have access to a drill/driver, use a standard power drill and bit set to drill the numerous holes you'll need for mounting the drawer fronts, doors, and hardware.

LAMINATE TRIMMER WITH FLUSH-TRIM BIT. This is the best tool for trimming veneer and end panels. The diminutive size of the router lets it go places its larger cousins can't.

PUTTY & PUTTY KNIFE. Fill old hardware holes in face frames using putty and a putty knife.

CIRCULAR OR SABER SAW. The panels that cover exposed cabinet ends will need to be cut to size. Likewise, you'll have to cut any molding to fit—use either a circular saw or saber saw.

SANDING BLOCK & 150-GRIT SANDPAPER. Smooth putty-filled holes flat with a sanding block wrapped with 150-grit sandpaper.

HANDSAW. You'll need a handsaw to trim the lips off the old drawer fronts if they're the three-sided variety (see DO IT RIGHT, p. 90).

TRISODIUM PHOSPHATE (TSP). Use this solution to clean your cabinets before refacing.

GLUE OR CONSTRUCTION ADHESIVE. Either works well for attaching end panels to cabinets.

CLAMPS. Use spring clamps and a wooden cleat to ensure uniform height on all your doors.

❖ COOL TOOL

Although it's used primarily to bond plastic laminate to countertops, a laminate roller is an ideal tool for pressing self-adhesive veneer in place. A metal handle coupled with a hard rubber roller lets you exert firm, even pressure to guarantee a good bond. If you don't have a laminate roller, your best bet is to use an ordinary rolling pin.

⊘ UPGRADE

There's no better time to upgrade your cabinets with distinctive molding and trim than when you're refacing. Most refacing suppliers offer decorative matching trim such as crown molding, dentil molding, and even decorative valences for over your kitchen sink or range.

What to Buy

1| SELF-ADHESIVE VENEER. The self-adhesive veneer sold by most refacing suppliers comes in large, flexible rolls, typically 24 in. by 96 in. The general rule of thumb for ordering rolls is you'll need one roll for roughly every 10 doors. So if you have 25 doors, you'll need three rolls.

2| DOORS & DRAWER FRONTS. The doors and drawer fronts for your cabinets will have to be made to fit your kitchen. Since these are custom parts, expect to wait 3 to 5 weeks for delivery. Follow the manufacturer's ordering directions and double-check your order before placing it. You won't get a refund on a custom order. Use the screws recommended by the manufacturer to attach the drawer fronts.

3| END PANELS (IF NECESSARY). In most kitchens, one or more of the cabinets will be exposed on the end. These are covered with matching panels, typically ¼-in. hardwood plywood, that you'll cut to fit. It's available in a variety of sizes to cover base, wall, and pantry-type cabinets.

4| MOLDING. If you don't want to add decorative molding, you'll likely need some simple cove and/or quarter-round moldings to serve as transitions between your cabinets and the adjacent walls and ceiling. Most refacing suppliers stock a variety of shapes and sizes of moldings finished to match the other refacing supplies.

5| HINGES. You can reuse your old hinges, but now's a good time to pick up some new ones for a fresh look. If your old doors required a catch to keep the door closed, consider upgrading to self-closing hinges—no catch required.

6| DOOR & DRAWER PULLS. In general, knobs are used for doors and pulls for drawers. But it's your kitchen, so you can do whatever you want (see Design Options, pp. 92-95, for more on hardware options).

DO IT RIGHT

The most common, and costly, mistake when refacing cabinets is ordering wrong-size parts. To avoid this, you must measure accurately, carefully compile a list of what you'll need, and then double-check it. Start by making a rough sketch of the kitchen cabinets. Label each with an alphanumeric code starting with "W" for wall cabinets and "B" for base cabinets. Follow the refacing manufacturer's directions for measuring doors and drawers. Most will ask you to measure the openings, and then add a specified amount to each measurement. Record the opening size for each cabinet, then add the designated amount. Double-check your measurements and your math before placing your order.

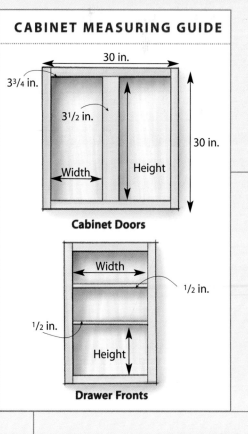

CABINET MEASURING GUIDE

30 in.

3¾ in.

3½ in.

30 in.

Width

Height

Cabinet Doors

Width

½ in.

½ in.

Height

Drawer Fronts

Reface the Cabinets

1 **REMOVE THE OLD DOORS & DRAWERS.** The first step to giving your cabinet a new face is to pull out the drawers and remove the old doors. A drill/driver fitted with a screwdriver bit will make quick work of removing the doors. Label the drawers with a pencil mark on bottom so you'll know where to return them after you've put on the new fronts.

2 **PREP THE SURFACES.** Once you remove the doors, you'll need to prep the face frames before you apply the veneer. Start by filling any old hardware mounting holes with putty, leaving it a bit proud of the hole. Once the putty has dried, sand it flat. Clean the surface with a mild solution of TSP, following the manufacturer's directions. Allow this to dry and then scuff sand the face frame with sandpaper wrapped around a sanding block. You're not trying to remove the old surface here, just roughen it up slightly to give the adhesive on the veneer something to "grab" onto.

3 **ATTACH THE END PANELS & TRIM.** Cover the exposed cabinet ends with 1/4-in. matching plywood panels. Measure carefully and cut the plywood slightly oversize with a circular saw. Apply glue or a bead of construction adhesive to the back of the panel about 2 in. in from the  edge around the perimeter of the panel. Attach the panel to the cabinet with brads and a hammer. Then use a block plane or laminate trimmer to trim the edges of the panels flush with the face frame.

4 **APPLY VENEER TO THE STILES.** Apply veneer to the vertical portions of the face frames (the stiles) first. Measure each stile and cut a piece of veneer roughly 1/2 in. to 3/4 in. wider and 2 in. longer than your measurement. Then cut the veneer to size with scissors. Peel off the backing and carefully center the veneer on the stile. Press the veneer in place with a laminate roller. Repeat for all the remaining stiles. When done, go back and trim off excess veneer with a utility knife. The edges of the stile will act as a straightedge to guide your cuts.

1

2

3

4

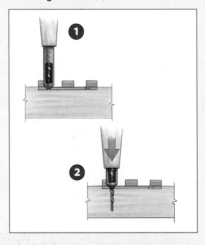

Add Doors & Drawer Fronts

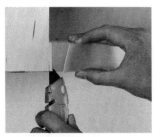

5 **APPLY VENEER TO THE RAILS & TRIM.** Measure and cut veneer for the horizontal pieces (the rails) just as you did for the stiles. Again, cut the pieces 1/2 in. to 3/4 in. wider and 2 in. longer than needed. Apply veneer to the rails, following the steps you used for the stiles. Now position a combination square so its blade is aligned with the inside edge of the stile. Then use a utility knife to cut through the overlapping layers of veneer on the rail and stile. Carefully peel the end of the rail piece back and remove the waste underneath. Press the rail end back to create a flawless joint. Repeat for all rail pieces.

6 **REMOVE OLD DRAWER FRONTS.** If your drawers are four-sided, remove the screws that hold on the "false" front. If the false front is held in place with brads, use a prybar and hammer to remove it. If your drawers are three-sided, cut off the drawer lips (see DO IT RIGHT, left).

7 **ATTACH NEW DRAWER FRONTS.** To attach each new drawer front, first drill oversize holes in the inside front of the drawer. (If applicable, you can reuse the existing screw holes.) Drive two screws through these holes to attach the new front. Leave the screws friction-tight. Install the drawer in the cabinet, check the alignment, and tighten the screws after making any necessary adjustments.

8 **ATTACH THE DOORS.** Mount the hinges (see "Painted Cabinets," step 8, p. 22). To ensure that all doors are installed at the same height, clamp a cleat (use a section of a 1x2) to the bottom of the first cabinet. Set a door on the cleat, center it, and drill holes for the mounting screws. Drive the screws in. Repeat for the remaining doors.

9 **ADD HARDWARE.** Measure each drawer and door for the hardware, mark the location, and then drill the holes for knobs and pulls. Attach the knobs and pulls using the hardware provided.

5 **6**

7 **8**

9

The clean lines of the doors and drawers and the inviting warmth of cherry give this kitchen a simple Shaker look. The dark-toned, understated hardware complements both the countertop hue and the feel of the kitchen.

Creating a new look for your kitchen doesn't have to involve a lot of time or a lot of money. In lieu of a major renovation, simply try a little face-lift. Updating the drawer fronts and faces on your old cabinets can make your kitchen look brand new again. Switch out worn knobs and pulls for more up-to-date ceramic, metal, or hand-painted designs. Mix and match to create your own personal statement.

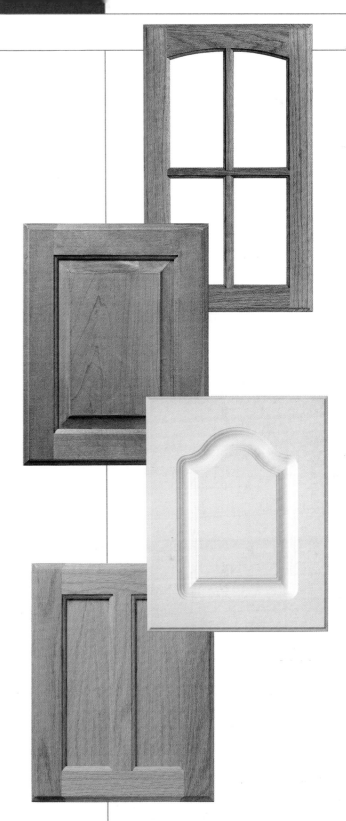

The hardest part of refacing cabinets just might be choosing the right doors. Traditional or contemporary, light or dark, there are door styles and finishes to suit any taste.

Reflecting the history, heritage, and culture of native North America, these knobs and pulls are inspired by totem art and the natural beauty of the Pacific Northwest.

Upgrade your hinges when you replace cabinet doors. Four types (from top): cup type, no-adjustment type, adjustable, and traditional butt hinge.

Nothing "heavy" about these metals: from classic simplicity to unexpected whimsy, whether shiny or matte-finished, this hardware is anything but ordinary.

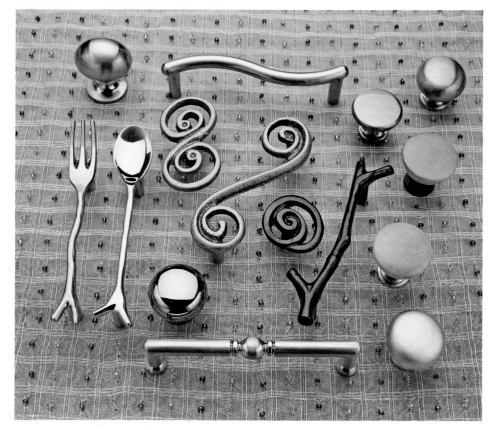

Here are just three of the myriad refacing woods and styles available (clockwise from left): cherry frame-and-panel, unfinished paint-grade maple, and pickled maple.

A beadboard finish and glass door fronts give this kitchen an updated country look. The light cabinets and walls make this cheery room seem larger than it is.

Island on Wheels

Assemble this **KITCHEN ISLAND** from stock cabinets and a premade countertop for instant storage and workspace

ET'S SEE A SHOW OF HANDS: Whose kitchen has enough storage and counter space? If your hand is down, you can solve both those problems with this simple, low-cost addition. This kitchen island is made up of two inexpensive, ready-made cabinets and a custom-made top to give you instant storage and instant workspace. Add wheels and your island can go anywhere—roll it out onto the deck or patio for summer serving or use it as an impromptu buffet table or serving cart in the dining room.

ADD ROLLERS   CONNECT THE CABINETS   ADD THE END PANELS   PUT ON A TOP

The most reliable way to match your kitchen island to your cabinets is to remove one of your existing doors and take it to a local home center. One of the kitchen pros there can match it to the cabinets the store carries.

LINGO

There are two basic types of castors: fixed and swivel. Fixed castors allow for travel in only one direction. Swivel castors can pivot, allowing travel in any direction. Most carts and rolling equipment feature one pair of each—typically with fixed castors in the front and swivel castors in the rear. For maximum rigidity, all the castors in your island should be the locking variety in which a brake pad or arm presses up against the wheel to lock it in place when engaged.

Tools & Gear

The basic carpentry tools listed below are all that you need to build a rolling island.

TAPE MEASURE. The back and end panels need to be cut to fit from plywood. A 12-ft. tape measure is all you'll need to accurately measure the cabinets for these parts.

DRILL OR CORDLESS DRILL/DRIVER & BITS. The cabinets are fastened together and the top is attached to the cabinets with screws. A drill and screwdriver will do the job, or you can use a drill/driver to drill holes and drive in screws. Depending on how your castors mount, you'll probably need to drill holes for them as well. See the manufacturer's instructions for recommended bit sizes.

CIRCULAR OR SABER SAW. The best way to cut the plywood back and end panels to size is with a circular or saber saw.

HANDSAW & MITER BOX. If you need to add any trim, it's best to cut it to length with a handsaw and a miter box. You can also use a handsaw to cut plywood to size if you don't have access to a circular or saber saw.

HAMMER, NAIL SET, PUTTY & PUTTY KNIFE. The back and end panels are attached to the cabinets with glue and brads. You'll need a nail set to drive the brads below the surface before applying putty.

CLAMPS. A pair of clamps (any type, as along as they can span at least 2 in.) will come in handy to temporarily hold the cabinets together while you drive in screws.

CONSTRUCTION ADHESIVE OR GLUE. You'll need construction adhesive or wood glue for attaching the back and end panels to the cabinet.

COOL TOOL

A cordless trim saw is the perfect tool for cutting plywood and small trim. It combines lightweight and cord-free operation to make fast, accurate cuts. Trim saws are available for rent from many home or rental centers.

What to Buy

1| CABINETS. We used two cabinets for our island. Most home centers stock ready-made cabinets in oak. If you want other styles or finishes, you'll need to order cabinets. Another option is to purchase RTA (ready-to-assemble) cabinets and put them together yourself. They are usually available in numerous configurations and finishes.

2| HARDWARE. You can either order hardware that matches your existing knobs and pulls or go with a completely different look as an accent.

3| PLYWOOD. The ends and backs of kitchen cabinets are unfinished. Since your island will be exposed on all sides, you'll need to cover the ends and back with matching plywood. Hardwood plywood (typically oak and birch) can be found at most home centers. Select 1/4-in. plywood that matches the wood of your island cabinets and then buy stain to match the plywood to the cabinets' color. Protect the stained wood with a few coats of polyurethane.

4| CASTORS. Pick up two sets of locking castors: one pair fixed, the other pair swivel. Most castors mount by either a baseplate that is secured with screws or a shaft that snaps into a toothed flange. Either type will work fine for your island. Try to find heavy-duty castors with rubber-coated wheels. These castors can handle heavy loads and will roll smoothly on most kitchen floors.

5| COUNTERTOP. Bring the overall dimensions of your cabinets to most home centers, and the kitchen design pros there will tell you what size countertop you'll need. They'll also help you through the myriad material choices available. Be prepared to wait 4 to 6 weeks for your top to be made and delivered.

6| 2x4 LUMBER. The bottoms of most cabinets are not thick enough to fully support castors. One solution is to attach 2x4 blocking to the underside of the cabinet and mount the castors to these. The amount of lumber you'll need depends on the cabinet depth. We used two 18-in.- to 20-in.-long pieces of a 2x4 on our island.

7| L-BRACKETS. Most countertops will attach to the cabinets via a set of four L-brackets screwed to the inside faces of the cabinets. Solid-surface tops are best attached with a generous bead of silicone caulk around the top of the cabinets to adhere the top to the base.

8| WOOD CORNER TRIM. Conceal the exposed plywood edges on the island back and ends with 3/4-in.-square matching corner trim. You'll need about 10 ft. of trim to cover all four corners.

DO IT NOW

It's important to leave plenty of clearance around your island for normal work and traffic flow. Kitchen designers suggest a minimum of 36 in. on all sides. Use masking tape to lay out your tentative island profile on the floor. Measure from the profile to surrounding cabinets and appliances to ensure sufficient clearance.

Castor & Cabinet Assembly

1 **REMOVE THE CABINET DOORS & DRAWERS.** To make your cabinets lighter and less cumbersome to maneuver, temporarily remove the doors and drawers.

2 **CUT & ATTACH THE CASTOR BLOCKING.** Most castors are not high enough to clear the recess in the bottom of the cabinets—if you mounted them to the cabinet bottom they wouldn't extend out far enough to touch the floor. You'll need to attach blocking to the cabinet bottoms to position the castors properly and provide a better foundation for the castors. Flip the cabinets over and measure and cut two lengths of 2x4 to fit between the toekick and cabinet back. Secure these to the inside faces of the two outside cabinet ends with glue and screws.

3 **ATTACH THE CASTORS.** Drill mounting holes in the blocking for the castors. Attach the castors to the blocking either by screwing the baseplates to the blocking or by snapping the castor shafts into the toothed flanges that you've driven into the mounting holes.

4 **ASSEMBLE THE CABINETS.** Flip the cabinets right side up and temporarily fasten them together with clamps. Drill pilot holes and drive screws through one cabinet side and into the other. Install three screws along each top and along the inside faces of the cabinets.

5 **LAY OUT & CUT THE END PANELS.** Measure each end and cut the plywood to size. You'll also need to cut a notch at the bottom front corner of each panel for the toekick. First, lay out the cut by clamping the plywood to the cabinet end and tracing around the notch with a pencil. Then cut the plywood to length. Apply finish to the panels (see DO IT FAST, left) and let them dry. Then apply construction adhesive or glue 2 in. in from the edges around the perimeter of the panels. Attach them to the cabinet ends with brads.

To make your nails invisible, first set them below the surface by tapping a nail set gently with a hammer. Then go back and fill in the depressions with matching putty.

The toekick is the flat piece below the notched front edge of the cabinets. This space allows you to stand close to the cabinets for food preparation and other tasks. On all cabinets, the toekick is unfinished. Fortunately, it's easy to conceal this unfinished area by cutting a strip of hardwood plywood that matches your cabinet and attaching it to the toekick with brads and glue.

Add the Back & the Top

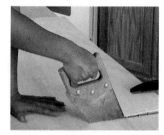

6 **CUT & ATTACH THE BACK.** Once the end panels are in place, you can add the back. Measure the back of the island, lay out the measurements on the plywood, and cut a piece to length. Just as you did with the end panels, apply glue 2 in. in from the edges around the perimeter of the plywood and attach it to the island back. Hammer 1-in. brads every 6 in. to 8 in. around the perimeter.

7 **HIDE THE EXPOSED PLYWOOD EDGES.** You'll need to cover the edges of the plywood back with ³/₄-in. by ³/₄-in. corner trim. Measure and cut the trim to length. Apply a bead of construction adhesive down the center of the inside face of the trim. The adhesive will spread out to both faces once the molding is pressed into position on the corner. Use masking tape or duct tape to hold the trim in place until the adhesive sets up—usually overnight.

8 **ATTACH THE COUNTERTOP.** The island is complete except for the top. If you're using L-brackets to secure the top to the island, first attach them to the inside faces of the cabinet ends. Then position the top on the island so that it's centered from front to back and from side to side. Secure the top by driving screws up through the brackets (you'll need two screws for each bracket) and into the top.

9 **REPLACE THE DOORS & DRAWERS AND ADD HARDWARE.** Finally, remount the doors and drawers. Add knobs and pulls, if desired, to match your existing cabinet hardware.

6 **7**

8 **9**

Design an island that works for you. This open shelf with hanging rods allows pots and pans to be accessible when needed, but out of your way when they're not.

If you don't want to wait the couple of weeks it takes to get most cabinets delivered, consider RTA (ready-to-assemble) cabinets. This island features two 15-in. drawer bases and one 18-in. door/drawer unit. It's topped off by a custom-made maple butcher block.

When it comes to multitasking, nothing beats a kitchen

island. This unit will provide you with extra space for food prep, storage, and even eating—all without breaking out a wall. The material options are endless: Put a laminate or wood top over your choice of cabinets, add wheels or make it stationary, and finish as you like. You'll just love having your own private island.

With its harmonizing, cool blue tones, this ample island looks like it belongs right where it is. The countertop was made oversize to provide an extended lip for extra seating.

Cost-efficient, durable, easy-to-clean laminate is a great choice for island tops. The tough part is choosing from the hundreds of colors and patterns available today.

End-unit bookshelves enhance the storage power of this island while giving the unit the look of furniture.

Laminate Tile Floor

Get a NEW FLOOR in a snap with laminate flooring that LOOKS LIKE TILE

TEMPTED BY CERAMIC TILE but turned off by the cost? Let laminate flooring give you the look you want—without the aspects you don't—for your new kitchen floor. Hardworking laminate mimics almost any material you can put under foot: tile, of course, plus hardwood, stone, slate, and more. Laminate easily takes the use—and abuse—of kitchen life, and you can install it over almost any other flooring (except carpeting). With snap-together assembly, installation takes little time, and the result is high impact.

LAY THE UNDERLAYMENT   SNAP TOGETHER FLOORING   INSTALL TRANSITION STRIPS   FINISH OFF WITH TRIM

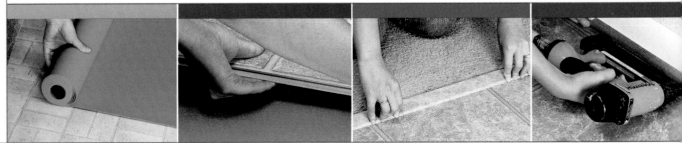

Tools & Gear

Installing laminate flooring requires only basic carpentry tools, plus a few specialty items.

PRYBAR, PUTTY KNIVES & PUTTY. Most flooring manufacturers recommend removing existing baseboard before installing laminate flooring. To keep from harming your walls, this is best done with a prybar and a pair of putty knives, one with a wide blade. You'll also need to fill in any nail holes in your trim with putty.

TAPE MEASURE. Measure twice, cut once. A 12-in. tape measure will handle all your measuring needs here.

COMPASS AND/OR CONTOUR GAUGE (OPTIONAL). If you need to cut flooring to fit around any obstacles (such as a pipe or molding), you can scribe the flooring to fit with a compass, or define the shape with a contour gauge.

RUBBER MALLET & TAPPING BLOCK. Even snap-together flooring requires the occasional whack to create a tight joint. Have a rubber mallet on hand and either buy or rent the tapping block recommended by the manufacturer. A tapping block is milled to match the profile of the flooring so it won't damage the flooring.

HANDSAW, MITER BOX & HACKSAW. Instead of cutting around door casings, it's easier to undercut the molding so the flooring can slip under it. A handsaw and a scrap of flooring are all you'll need for the job. Use a handsaw with a miter box to cut trim. If the transition moldings you're installing use a metal track, you'll need a hacksaw to cut it to length.

UTILITY KNIFE OR SCISSORS. Either of these trusty tools can easily cut most underlayment.

CIRCULAR OR SABER SAW. Laminate flooring is tough to cut with a handsaw. Consider buying, renting, or borrowing a circular or saber saw.

SCREWDRIVER, CORDLESS DRILL/DRIVER & BITS. Depending on your subfloor, you might need to drill pilot holes for mounting transition strips. Transition strips are generally screwed to the subfloor. You can do this with a screwdriver or, more preferably, a drill/driver fitted with a screwdriver bit.

SNAP TOGETHER

TONGUE AND GROOVE

WHAT'S DIFFERENT?

When laminate flooring was first introduced, the edges of planks were cut with matching tongue-and groove joints. The parts were held together by glue applied at the joint. Although the profiles milled in the edges of snap-together planks resemble a tongue-and-groove joint, there are additional ridges and valleys that force the mating pieces to snap tightly together when assembled.

What to Buy

1| UNDERLAYMENT & SEAM TAPE. You'll need to install underlayment before laying down any laminate flooring. Laminate flooring manufacturers offer a variety of options for this—rolls of foam are the most common. It's important to select the correct type for your subfloor (see WHAT'S DIFFERENT, p. 110). Also, most manufacturers recommend using their brand-specific tape to seal the strips of underlayment together.

2| LAMINATE FLOORING. Most laminate flooring is made up of four layers. The top, or wear, layer is cellulose paper that's impregnated with clear melamine resins. Under this is the design layer (a photo or other pattern printed on paper). The middle layer, or core, is usually fiberboard. The bottom, or stability, layer works along with the top layer to create a moisture barrier to help keep the core from warping. Because the core is wood, it's important to buy your flooring in advance of the intended installation date so the planks can acclimate to the room. Most manufacturers recommend placing unopened cartons of flooring in the room where they'll be installed at least 72 hours in advance.

3| TRANSITION MOLDINGS & TRIM. You'll need a transition strip wherever your new laminate flooring meets other flooring. For laminate flooring these are usually two-part units: a metal or plastic track that is attached to the subfloor, and a strip that snaps into the track to create a smooth transition. Strips are available to transition to carpet, wood flooring, vinyl, and ceramic tile. Also, whether you removed your old base trim or not, you'll still need some type of trim to conceal the expansion gap between the flooring and wall or old base trim.

4| INSTALLATION KIT. Some manufacturers offer kits to make installing their floors easier. Some you can buy and others can be checked out like a library book and returned when the job is finished. Contents usually include a tapping block, a pull bar for pulling planks together at the ends, expansion spacers, and special clamps (if required).

COOL TOOL

Sure, **you can cut** laminate flooring with a handsaw and a miter box, but a power miter saw will make quick, accurate cuts with little effort. If you don't want to lay out the dough to buy one, you can rent one from most home and rental centers.

DO IT RIGHT

Most **manufacturers** recommend that you use glue with their snap-together flooring when used on kitchen floors. Water and food spills are common here, and gluing the joints creates a watertight seal that keeps out moisture that can cause the joints to swell.

✦ **DO IT NOW**

Your subfloor should be level and free from dips and high spots. Check this with a 4-ft. level at various points in the room. Any depression greater than 3/16 in. should be filled with a leveling compound—a cement-based coating that goes down smoothly and sets up quickly. Most compounds are ready for the next step in the installation process in less than an hour.

⊛ **WHAT'S DIFFERENT?**

All underlayment is not the same. Closed-cell polyethylene is the most common underlayment for laminate floors. It provides fair cushioning and noise reduction, but offers no barrier to moisture. If you're installing laminate flooring over a concrete floor or over a subfloor that has an uninsulated crawl space below, you'll need a vapor retarder to keep moisture from rising up into the flooring. You can buy either separate sheet plastic for this, or a 2-in-1 foam underlayment, which combines a vapor retarder with a foam cushion.

Prep the Old Floor

1 **REMOVE THE BASEBOARD.** Most manufacturers recommend removing your old baseboard before installing flooring. This can be done with a wide-blade putty knife and a prybar. Slip the putty knife behind the baseboard and insert the prybar between the knife and the  trim. The putty knife will prevent the prybar from damaging your wall as you pull off the base. If you plan on reusing the baseboard, use two putty knives and sandwich the prybar between them. The second putty knife will protect the baseboard.

2 **UNDERCUT THE TRIM AT DOORWAYS.** The next step to prepare for laminate flooring is to undercut the door casings. Place a scrap of laminate flooring on the existing floor to serve as a guide. Lay your handsaw down flat on the scrap and cut through the trim. This will create the perfect gap for the new flooring to slip under.

3 **CLEAN THE FLOOR THOROUGHLY.** Once you're done making sawdust, use a vacuum to thoroughly clean the floor. Go over it twice, because even small bits of debris trapped under the foam underlayment can cause problems down the road.

4 **INSTALL THE FOAM UNDERLAYMENT.** Place the cut end of the foam underlayment roll against the wall in one corner of the room and unroll it. Cut it to length with a sharp utility knife or a pair of scissors. To prevent tearing the underlayment as you work, most manufacturers suggest laying one row of foam at a time and then covering it with flooring.

5 **TAPE THE SEAMS.** When it's time to join together strips of foam underlayment, butt the edges together and use the recommended tape to join the seams. Make sure the foam doesn't overlap.

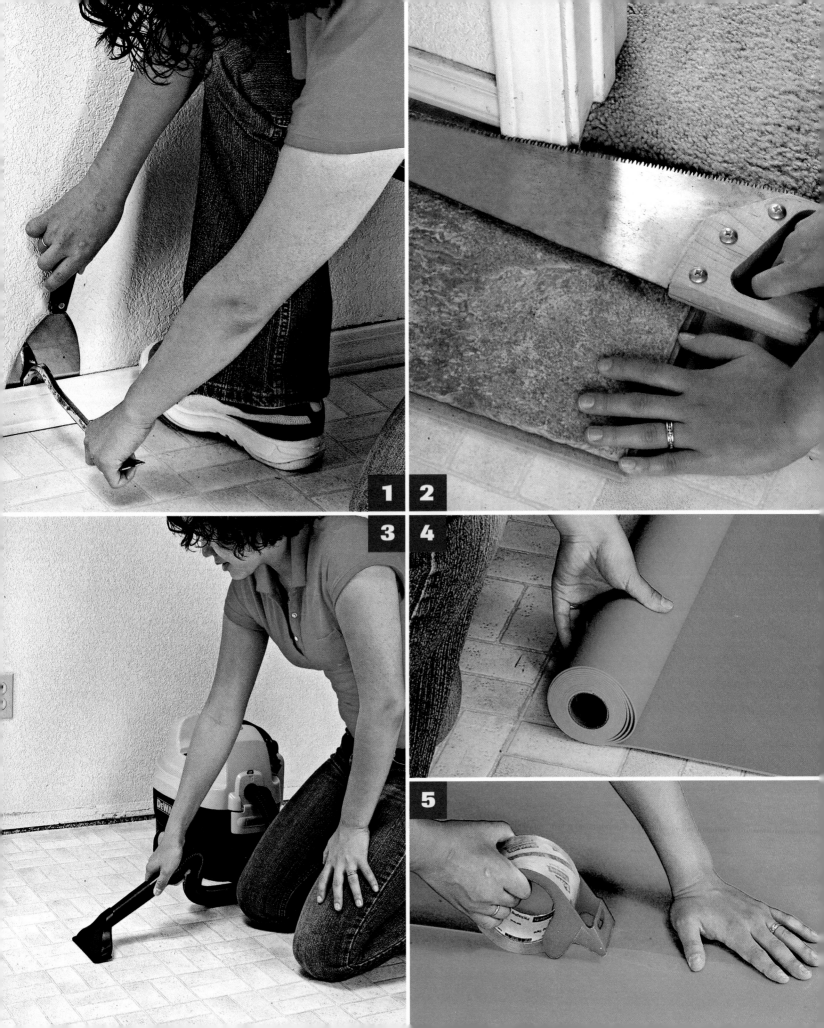

Until they're assembled, the edges of laminate flooring are delicate—so delicate that they're easily dinged during shipment or installation. Before installing any plank, first check the edges to make sure they're pristine. Any damage can prevent planks from fitting together properly.

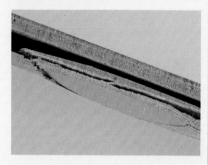

Laminate flooring needs gaps around its perimeter so it can expand and contract as the seasons change. The most reliable way to create this gap is to use spacers— either provided in the installation kit or made from scraps of wood.

Lay the Floor Tiles

6 **FORM LONG STRIPS.** Both the long edges and the ends of laminate planks snap together. This means you'll have to connect all the planks in a row together end-to-end before you can snap the long edges together. Starting at one wall, snap the planks together until you near the opposite wall. Measure the gap, cut a partial plank, and snap it in place. Make sure to leave the recommended gap at both ends of the strip.

7 **POSITION THE FIRST STRIP.** Now slide the long strip against the wall, taking care to place spacers every 8 in. to 10 in. and at the end of every plank. Double-check to make sure you've left the appropriate gap at the ends of the strip.

8 **STAGGER THE JOINTS.** Follow the manufacturer's instructions for staggering the joints. The most common method is to cut the first plank in the second row so it's roughly two-thirds the length of a full plank. The first plank in the third row is cut one-third the length of a full plank. Be sure to cut the end of the plank that butts up against the wall. Form a long strip and snap this onto the first strip. Continue cutting and snapping planks until you reach an obstacle or the opposite wall.

9 **MARK AROUND OBSTACLES.** You can use a compass to "scribe" around an obstacle, or use a contour gauge to create a template of the obstacle. To scribe with a compass, place a plank as close as possible to the wall. Open the compass so it spans the largest gap between the plank and wall. Set the pencil on the plank and press the point of the compass against the wall. As you guide the compass along the wall, the pencil will copy irregularities onto the plank.

10 **CUT THE PLANKS AS NEEDED.** Clamp the marked plank to a sawhorse and cut to size with a handsaw, saber saw, or circular saw. For curved cuts, the saber saw works best. To fit the plank around an obstacle (such as a pipe) you'll need to cut it in half at the center of the obstacle, then fit each half around the obstacle.

You can miter trim where it meets at a corner, but you'll get a better fit if you make a coped joint. Measure the length of the piece you'll need, then add the thickness of the molding to this measurement and cut a piece to length. For example, if the wall is 80 in. long and you're using ³/₄-in. molding, cut the piece 80³/₄ in. long. Next, cut the end of the molding to be coped at a 45-degree angle with a handsaw and a miter box. This will expose the molding profile. Then cut into the mitered end with a coping saw, following the curved profile (below).

A brad nailer will make quick work of installing trim. This air-powered hammer will drive and set a brad in the blink of an eye. You can rent an air nailer and compressor at most home centers and rental centers.

Add Transition Strips

11 **LAY THE FINAL PLANKS.** When you've laid all the full planks you can and you're near the opposite wall from where you started, you'll likely be left with a space that's not wide enough for a full plank. Measure the distance between the last full board and the wall and cut a plank to fit with a circular or saber saw. As you cut the planks to width, take care to leave an expansion gap.

12 **INSTALL THE TRANSITION TRACK.** Once all the flooring is in place, follow the manufacturer's instructions for cutting the metal or plastic track to fit inside the door opening. Then position the track as directed and fasten it to the subfloor with the screws recommended by the manufacturer.

13 **INSTALL THE TRANSITION STRIP.** With the track in place, follow the manufacturer's directions to cut the transition strip to length. To install the strip, simply position it over the track and snap it in place. Some strips can be stubborn: You may need a rubber mallet to "persuade" them to fit into the track.

14 **ADD THE BASE TRIM.** If you're reinstalling the baseboard, now's the time to nail it back on. To complete the floor, you'll need to add trim to conceal the expansion gap between the flooring and the walls. Measure and cut trim with a handsaw and miter box. Fasten the trim to the wall or existing baseboard with a hammer and nails or with an air nailer (see COOL TOOL, left). When all the trim is in place, fill any nail holes with matching putty.

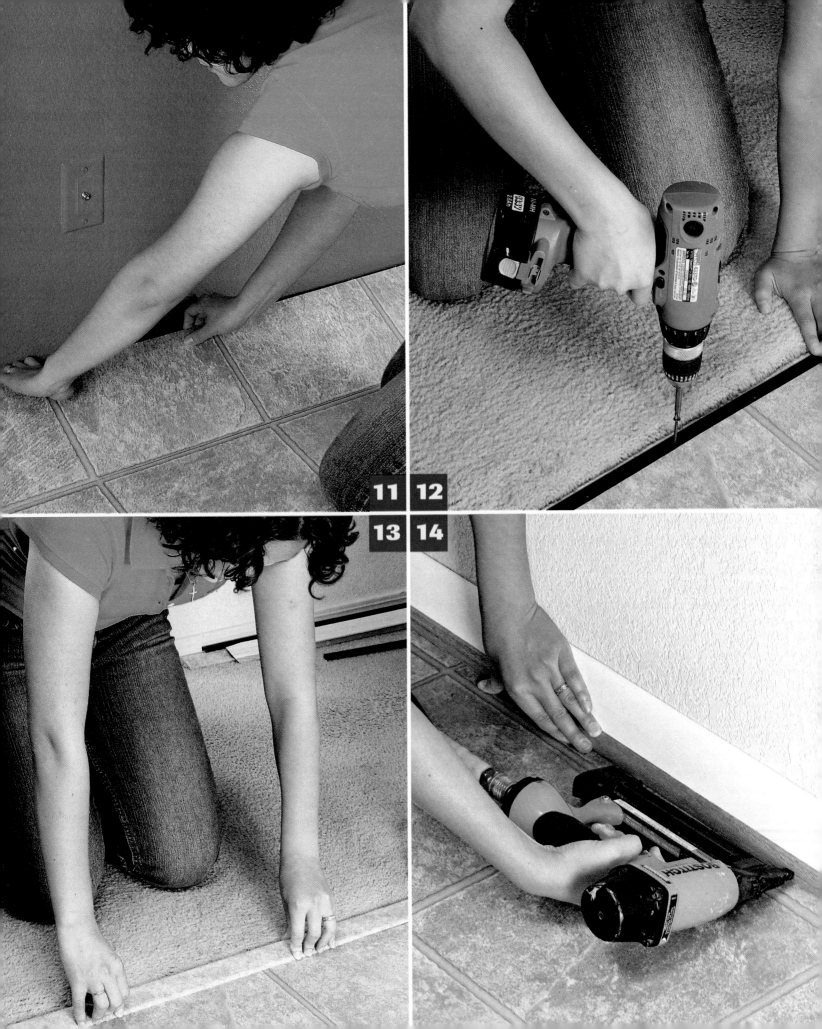

Fancy or fundamental, kitchen floors are made to take daily abuse in stride and still look good. Whether you want the look of wood, tile, or stone, an intricate pattern or a simple design, manufacturers have you covered. There are even options in transition strips and underlayment, so step right up and make your selections.

Quality vinyl flooring is available in colors and patterns (inlaid for durability) galore.

This ceramic tile look-alike is really a patterned laminate. Other laminates mimic stone and concrete or are patterned.

This isn't your grandmother's linoleum. It's made from natural ingredients, but doesn't try to mimic any other substance. And color options are practically limitless! You can even add a decorative border.

Many types of underlayment are available to fit varying subfloors and foundations. Depending on your subflooring, you can choose (from left): a cushioned underlayment with moisture barrier, a foam cushion only, or a cushion with moisture barrier and noise reducer.

You can find laminate flooring that mimics just about any wood type and finish.

Love the look of wood but not the cost or care? Try laminate flooring. This single-wide plank design has beveled edges on all four sides that create a unique V-groove between planks.

Many transition strips are designed to snap into a U-shaped track (far left). All five common types are made to match the laminate flooring (from left): stair nosing to finish stair edges; T-molding to join two laminate floors; carpet transitions to go from laminate to carpeting; end molding to finish laminate flooring at sliding doors, ceramic tiles, and other areas; hard surface reducers to transition between laminate flooring and lower hard surface floors such as vinyl, wood, or tile.

The wide array of ceramic tiles lets you create your own custom patterns, looks, and themes. Just take your time with installation for lasting looks and performance.

Tile patterns really "pop" in an otherwise solid-colored kitchen. A border defines both the range area and the room's perimeter.

Photo Credits

All photos appearing in this book are by Christopher Vendetta, except:

p. 24: (top) © Turnstyle Designs, Ltd.; (bottom) © The Taunton Press, Inc., photo by Roe A. Osborn

p. 25: (top left) © Turnstyle Designs, Ltd.; (right) © Povy Kendal Atchison; (bottom) © The Taunton Press, Inc., photo by Scott Phillips

p. 26: (left) Photo courtesy of Wellborn Cabinet, Inc.; (top) Liberty Hardware Manufacturing Corporation 1-800-542-3789/ www.libertyhardware.com; (right) © Kraftmaid Cabinetry 1-800-571-1990 www.kraftmaid.com

p. 27: (left and top right) © Liberty Hardware Manufacturing Corporation 1-800-542-3789/ www.libertyhardware.com; (bottom) © Turnstyle Designs, Ltd.

p. 36: (top left and top center) Photo courtesy of General Electric Company; (bottom left) © Stone Impressions; (bottom right) © DuPont™ Zodiaq® Quartz Surfaces

p. 37: (top left) © Stone Impressions; (top right) ©LG HI-MACS acrylic solid surface G01; (bottom left) © The Taunton Press, Inc., photo by Dan Thornton; (bottom right) © The Taunton Press, Inc., photo by Judi Rutz

p. 46: © Knape & Vogt Archives

p. 47: (left) © Kraftmaid Cabinetry 1-800-571-1990 www.kraftmaid.com; (right) © Knape & Vogt Archives

p. 48: © Kraftmaid Cabinetry 1-800-571-1990 www.kraftmaid.com

p. 49: © Kraftmaid Cabinetry 1-800-571-1990 www.kraftmaid.com

p. 58: (top left and top right) Photo courtesy American Standard, The Shadow Light Group, photographer; (bottom left and bottom right) Photo courtesy of American Standard, John Mowers, photographer

p. 59: © Photo courtesy of American Standard, Steve Henke, Henke Studio

p. 60: (left) Courtesy of Moen, Incorporated; (right) © Delta Faucet Company

p. 61: (top and center) Courtesy of Moen, Incorporated; (bottom) © Delta Faucet Company

p. 70: (left) © The Taunton Press, Inc., photo by Charles Bickford; (right) Photo courtesy of Progress Lighting

p. 71: (top left) © Brian Vanden Brink, photographer; (top right) Photo courtesy of Progress Lighting; (bottom right) © The Taunton Press, Inc., photo by Kevin Ireton

p. 72: Photo courtesy of Progress Lighting

p. 73: (top and right) Photo courtesy of Progress Lighting; (center) © The Taunton Press, Inc., photo by Charles Miller; (bottom) © The Taunton Press, Inc., photo by Scott Phillips

p. 92: © The Taunton Press, Inc., photo by Kevin Ireton

p. 93: (left) © Liberty Hardware Manufacturing Corporation 1-800-542-3789/ www.libertyhardware.com; (right top to bottom) Photos courtesy of Rockler.com

p. 94: (left top to bottom and bottom right) © The Taunton Press, Inc., photo by Scott Phillips; (top right) Liberty Hardware Manufacturing Corporation 1-800-542-3789/ www.libertyhardware.com

p. 95: © Ken Gutmaker

p. 104: (left) © Alloc, Inc./alloc.com

p. 105: (left) Courtesy of KitchenAid Home Appliances; (top right) © The Taunton Press, Inc., photo by Scott Phillips; (bottom) © Brian Vanden Brink, photographer

p. 116: (top left) © The Taunton Press, Inc., photo by Joseph Kugielsky; (right) © Wilsonart Flooring

p. 117: (top right) © The Taunton Press, Inc., photo by Joseph Kugielsky

p. 118: (center) © Alloc, Inc./alloc.com

p. 119: (left) © Chipper Hatter; (top right) © The Taunton Press, Inc., photo by Joseph Kugielsky

For more great weekend project ideas look for these and other
TAUNTON PRESS BOOKS wherever books are sold.

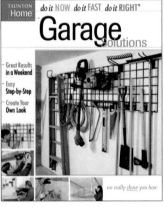

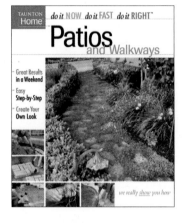

Bathroom Makeovers
ISBN 1-56158-727-3
Product #070798
$14.95 U.S.
$21.00 Canada

Garage Solutions
ISBN 1-56158-760-5
Product #070822
$14.95 U.S.
$21.00 Canada

Patios and Walkways
ISBN 1-56158-723-0
Product #070813
$14.95 U.S.
$21.00 Canada

Containers with Style
ISBN 1-56158-678-1
Product #070760
$14.95 U.S.
$21.00 Canada

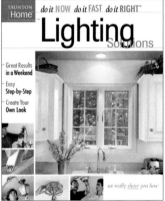

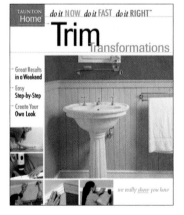

Paint Transformations
ISBN 1-56158-670-6
Product #070751
$14.95 U.S.
$21.00 Canada

Lighting Solutions
ISBN 1-56158-669-2
Product #070753
$14.95 U.S.
$21.00 Canada

Trim Transformations
ISBN 1-56158-671-4
Product #070752
$14.95 U.S.
$21.00 Canada

Storage Solutions
ISBN 1-56158-668-4
Product #070754
$14.95 U.S.
$21.00 Canada

For more information visit our Web site at www.doitnowfastright.com